STOP NURSE BURNOUT

What to Do When Working Harder Isn't Working

Elizabeth Scala MSN/MBA, RN
Co-authored with Dike Drummond, MD
Author of *Stop Physician Burnout*

CONTENTS

INTRODUCTION

"Be who you are and say what you feel,
for those who mind don't matter
and those who matter don't mind."
—Dr. Seuss

"Never mistake knowledge for wisdom.
One helps you make a living,
the other helps you make a life."
—Sandra Carey

WHAT YOU WILL FIND IN THIS BOOK

In 2011, I launched my website, elizabethscala.com, in an effort to help my nurse colleagues struggling with the changes in our modern healthcare system. A few weeks later, I received my first email from a burned-out nurse we will call Sally. She shared her feelings straight from the heart and was seeking support.

"I don't like my profession anymore," she wrote. "I'm disenchanted due to the politics and the paradigm shift the healthcare community has catapulted into … Press-Ganey instead of the greater good… tunnel-vision patient focus versus patient-nurse in a dynamic, working relationship. I have always connected with people, but I find too often I'm forced to be less than honest and hide my frustration with my job and the healthcare system. This isn't the nursing legacy I wanted to leave behind. I'm so exhausted from the toxicity—can you help me?"

As I read the email, I nodded along.

Unfortunately, I have heard this story many times since then. As nurses, we pride ourselves on the ability to work hard, soldier on, and keep going no matter what. This workaholic, "Lone Ranger" programming instilled over years of our nursing education is actually one of the core causes of burnout. This programming is so deep and wide, we can suffer severe burnout for years, only jolted into taking action when we can no longer deal with our extreme unhappiness at work.

My coaching work with overstressed nurses and the tools you will learn in this book are both inspired by this nurse and others who lost their lives, careers, and mar-

1

riages while under the influence of nurse burnout. Burnout is incredibly common. In an international survey of nurses, more than 40 percent of hospital staff nurses scored in the high range for job-related burnout, and more than 1 in 5 hospital staff nurses said they intended to leave their hospital jobs within one year.[1]

However, this type of workplace stress does have positive consequences. It motivated Sally to seek help, and she has recovered from her burnout after years of misery. Her request for coaching in the early days of elizabethscala.com allowed us to test the principles you will read in the pages ahead to ensure they worked in the real world.

This book is my attempt to reach all nurses with the tools you need to understand, detect, prevent, and treat burnout. As we learn about our common enemy, it can bring us together to support each other more effectively and change nurses' workaholic, "Lone Ranger," superhero culture.

Sally was the first of hundreds of nurses who have allowed me to support their recovery to a more ideal career and a more balanced life. We learned together what combination of tools would work to power her recovery.

This is one of the key learnings from my burnout work: burnout is always multifactorial. It has multiple overlapping causes.

- Sometimes, a dozen smaller stresses gang up on you, setting up the classic "death by a thousand paper cuts."
- In other cases, you are stressed at work, but the final blow is when something happens at home—a parent becomes ill and moves in, or your spouse moves out.
- Or, a tragic event at work can add to the usual stress of a busy practice to push you over the edge.

Everyone's burnout is different. Recovery is a process of switching out old habits with new ones, one at a time.

A systems approach is essential

That is what this book will teach you. You will see the systems of your life and career—and the overlap and interplay between them—in a new light. Like any ecosystem, changes in one system automatically affect the others. You can prevent burnout at work using actions you take at home. You can build more life balance with new actions you take at work.

In Sally's case, she was able to transition from a toxic workplace and severe burnout to a completely new position where she is happy, enjoys her career again, and gets to spend more time with her family and practicing yoga. She learned new tools to deal more effectively with stress at work. She built her Ideal Career Description and used it for a focused job search. She learned how to make sure her weeks were more balanced than before. She learned how to take her life and career back and begin living on purpose. A series of small changes combined to stop her downward spiral and enabled her to achieve a new place of satisfaction and fulfillment.

You can use this book to do the same thing.

FIELD-TESTED, NURSE-APPROVED TOOLS

Since the day Sally and I met in 2011, I have delivered thousands of hours of group coaching and online programs to nurses. As I write this, we have 2,400 nurses subscribed to the newsletter at elizabethscala.com. Our website and its library of free resources receives an average of six thousand visitors per month.

This ground level experience with nurses from all specialties has taught me what works with real nurses in real nursing careers. I call the contents of this book "field-tested and nurse-approved" because it is true. They will work for you too. With the tools in this book and the additional materials at our dedicated Resources Page at *StopNurseBurnout.com*, you can accomplish any or all of the following:

1.) Understand stress and burnout—most likely for the very first time.

There was no time to learn about burnout in nursing school or orientation. All the bandwidth was devoted to turning out a competent clinician. Unfortunately, the programming that puts us all at high-risk for burnout was instilled at the same time we were being molded into bright shiny young nurses.

And if that is not bad enough, I will wager you had several faculty members in nursing school who were the perfect example of the chronically overworked and burned-out nurse. They modeled the burned-out nurse rather than the professional with a fulfilling career and a well-balanced life.

This book will help you fill this gaping hole in your education once and for all. In Chapter 1, you will learn:

- Burnout symptoms and gender differences
- Burnout causes, effects, and pathophysiology
- How to recognize burnout in yourself and your colleagues
- What I believe to be burnout's highest and best use

2.) Learn how to prevent and treat your own burnout.

We will not stop at the point of comprehension. Understanding is never enough to actually reap the rewards of a new concept. Understanding is the booby prize. Understanding changes nothing until you put it to use by taking new actions.

Unfortunately, most nurses have been trained by decades in school to study a concept until we think we can answer a multiple-choice question on the topic. Typically, we study until we think we can pass the test. Then, we stop short of actually putting this new knowledge to use. Don't let this happen to you.

3.) Build a more Ideal Career and a more balanced life, no matter what.

If you are not suffering from burnout at the moment (though, perhaps you can see it coming if things don't change), I have good news. One of the fun things about these tools is they work for everyone, in every circumstance. They have unlimited upside.

You will learn tools to get crystal clear on your Ideal Career and always be moving in that direction. If you are suffering from burnout, you will recover. If you are doing just fine, you will be able to take your life and career to your next level of satisfaction and fulfillment with the very same techniques.

No matter where you start, you will learn to walk your personal path to a meaningful career and a fulfilling life with intention and purpose.

WHAT YOU WON'T FIND IN THIS BOOK

Untested theories and musing about things that *might* work.

Everything here is field-tested and nurse-approved—in *my* life and with hundreds of nurses in nearly every specialty and career circumstance.

A literature review, lengthy bibliography, or complicated academic discussion.

Burnout is prevented by taking different actions. Everything here is keyed on giving you new awareness and teaching new actions for immediate results. I will give you selected references for key points along the way, but don't let your built-in bias toward needing to "review the literature" slow you down.

Try this instead. Learn a tool, and then put it to use in the testing ground of your own life. See if it works for you. Your life is your research laboratory. I promise I won't teach you anything that has not worked for at least a hundred nurses before you.

I will continuously encourage you to take action. Try things out in your life. Do something new in order to get new results. If it works, keep doing it. If it doesn't work, move on. This is exactly what you ask your patients to do. Now, it is your turn. Time for action, not further research.

Complicated theories and named methodologies.

Have you ever noticed that the rules to live a great life are very, very simple? We are taught the most complex concepts on the planet in our nursing education, yet the principles of balance, happiness, and intention are all simple and easily understood. There is no rocket science here, but don't let that fool you.

- Clarity is power.
- Simplicity is power.
- More is not better.

Do not underestimate the ability of these straightforward tools and metaphors to help you take your life back, step by step. If you find yourself saying, "It *can't* be that simple," then try it out and prove it to yourself. I dare you to pick just one tool, put it into action, and see what happens.

Techniques that take a long time to pay off.

I am just a simple psychiatric nurse. If a technique does not provide you with a benefit on the day you first put it into action, it is not in here. Many of these tools can be learned in five minutes, put into action tomorrow, and provide you with benefits before you go to bed that night. But don't take my word for it. Pick a tool and take action.

WHICH BRINGS US BACK TO SALLY, MY FIRST COACHING CLIENT.

The principles gathered here are my attempt to ensure burnout never claims another victim like Sally. These tools were handed to me by my own experience and tested by hundreds of our brothers and sisters who fought their way back into the light to rebound from burnout. I am thrilled to pass them on to you.

HOW TO GET THE MOST OUT OF THIS BOOK

"To exist is to change, to change is to mature,
to mature is to go on creating oneself endlessly."
—Henri Bergson

"The way to get good ideas is to get lots of ideas
and throw the bad ones away."
—Linus Pauling

Disclaimer 1—this book is not just for nurses.

My work concentrates on nurses because I come from and operate in the world of nursing. They suffer a very high rate of burnout, making them an excellent group to study burnout symptoms, complications, and the tools for treatment and prevention.

At the same time, it is important to realize burnout affects all professions. No one is immune. Even though the burnout training that follows was developed by working with practicing nurses, it is applicable to—and appropriate for—anyone who is feeling stressed or burned-out by his or her job.

All who have direct patient contact as part of their usual job duties will benefit greatly from the discussion that follows: those within healthcare, physician's assistants, clinical technicians, doctors of all kinds—just substitute my use of the word *nurse* with your own career title, and you will find this teaching completely relevant. I have even had attorneys, dentists, veterinarians, healthcare executives, and even servers in restaurants tell me they learned valuable tools from this work.

Disclaimer 2—this book is just as useful if you are NOT burned out.

You can use the training and tools that follow to create a more Ideal Career and a more balanced life no matter how you feel about your work at the moment. If you are doing well, you can use the very same burnout prevention skills below to do even better. After all, your choice to become a nurse was meant to enable an extraordinary life. I will show you some field-tested ways to build that life, whether you are suffering from burnout or not.

FIVE KEYS TO ACCELERATE YOUR PROGRESS

1.) Read this book … and do not stop there.

I will assume you bought this book for a reason. There is most likely something about your career and your life you would like to change. For most people I meet, they look at the trajectory of their careers and don't like where things are headed. It is as if you have been on rails, like a train. You see where the tracks started and where they are headed, and continuing in this direction is no longer any fun at all. You have probably been feeling this way for a while. You would really like to step off of this set of tracks.

If you want to learn more about the cause and cure of this dissatisfaction, you are in the right place.

Much of the change you seek is hidden in the programming we all acquired in nursing school. Burnout prevention depends on learning how to recognize this programming and the automatic habits it spawns and how to wake up. Lift your head, take charge, and start switching those habits out for living on purpose.

If you want to actually change your career and your life, new awareness is mandatory and *not* sufficient all by itself. *Action* is the key.

I want to be very real with you here before we get started. Reading this book, if that is all you do, cannot help you make the changes you seek.

Consider Albert Einstein's definition of insanity:

> *"Insanity is doing the same things over and over*
> *and expecting a different result."*[2]
> —Albert Einstein

To get different results, *you must take different actions.*

Reading a book won't help until you use what you have learned to take different *actions* out in the real world.

This is why every section ends with ACTION STEPS. They are suggestions to put your new insights and tools to use immediately. Each of the dozens of actions work individually; the key is to pick one and do it. This is the only way to step out of the Groundhog Day that is the insanity definition.

2.) Journal.

Take notes as you read (in the margins is great!), AND I strongly recommend you also grab a journal to write down your insights and action steps. I will teach you things you don't know that you don't know, and though I love to write in the margins of good books, it limits you to short phrases of insight. There will be a number of times when the ideas below will have you journaling for several pages, if you are set up properly. Remember that insights are not action steps. You will have to go further than just a note or two in the margins if this book is to rise above the level of simple learning or entertainment.

I encourage you to buy a nice journal and use it as a companion to this book.

At the end of each chapter, make sure you also journal on the ACTION STEPS. Use your journal and the ACTION STEPS to explore how these new levels of awareness and new burnout prevention tools would make a difference in your career and your life.

Some of these passages will give words to things you have only experienced as feelings up until now. Write down your "ah-ha" moments and what new actions that "ah-ha" makes possible.

3.) Overview and prioritize.

I encourage you to read a chapter at a time as an overview. Journal on the concepts and how they apply to your situation. Then, go back and dive a little deeper into the points that are most relevant to you.

Read through the first chapter on Burnout Basics, and make notes in your journal on the ways burnout works in your life and your career. I have worked with hundreds of burned-out nurses, and I can assure you everyone's situation is unique. Your circumstances will not be a perfect match for any of your colleagues, although there is a small set of general themes.

Do not skip Chapter 2 on Head Trash. You must identify and take out the trash first before the tools that follow can sink in. Notice what flavors of head trash are most common in your inner dialogue.

Chapter 3 holds the most important concepts in this entire book:

- Your Ideal Career Description
- The Nurse's Venn of Happiness
- Your Master Plan

Read through the chapter so you can see how these key concepts reinforce each other. Then, create your version of all three. You will receive specific instructions on this process in the chapter.

Overview the entire tools section in Chapter 4 so you can see the whole scope of what we will cover before you put any of the tools into action. Some will apply to your situation and some will not. You get to pick favorites here. These are the building blocks for your own burnout prevention strategy.

4.) Share your insights with colleagues, friends, and family.

I encourage you to share what you learn—both in the book and about yourself—with nurse colleagues, staff members, your significant other, and anyone else who could be a part of your support system going forward. My experience is that learning, growing, personal development, and self-exploration are radically accelerated when you are having conversations with people who care about you along the way.

Your connection could also prompt them to make some positive changes in their own lives.

If you really want to take this process to a new level of fun and speed, consider forming a study group. One structure that works is to read a chapter a week and journal on it. Bring your journal to a monthly or weekly meeting of your study group—either in person or by phone or Skype—and share your insights and the action steps you will take in the week ahead.

You can become a mastermind group and mutual accountability buddies.

5.) Use the Power Tools Library to go deeper and wider.

Please understand that this book is the tip of an iceberg of over 117 field-tested ways to lower your stress and prevent burnout. The Power Tools Library at *StopNurseBurnout. com* is packed with additional tools, videos, audio downloads, and even a free Discovery Session consult to give you a personal strategic plan.

A written book like this one can only appeal to one learning style. The additional Power Tools allow us to expand these teachings to all your senses and gives you access to a comprehensive library of tools to build your ideal practice.

See the last chapter on Next Steps for the full listing of additional Power Tools.

This is an exclusive FREE library of additional Ideal Practice building tools and training at the web address below:

www.StopNurseBurnout.com/powertools

All of these additional Power Tools are free and my gift to you as an owner of this book.

Most of all, get ready to look at what it means to be a nurse in a whole new light. I want you to know there is no set of train tracks taking your career in a single, predetermined direction. The path you have been on is not set in stone. If you are ready to build your own Ideal Career and start living on purpose, it is time to get started.

But before we do that, I'd like to share with you my own story of being burned to the ground and how it came to pass that you are reading this book now.

MY BURNOUT STORY

THE LESSONS I share in this book were ones I started learning as my own nursing career came to a crashing halt in 2009, just shy of my five-year anniversary as a nurse. It was a category five hurricane, with my own lack of self-care at the eye of the storm.

I never wanted to be an R.N.

I suppose you need to go all the way back to when I was in college to find the start of my own burnout.

I was a party girl as an undergraduate. Six days a week, up all night, little sleep during the day. Sure, I went to class—I was good at passing tests. I also worked part time (I had to pay for my lifestyle, after all). When senior year came around and we were all discussing what we were going to do after graduation day, I allowed a group of roommates and my parents to decide my fate for me.

After graduating with my psychology degree, I was off to an accelerated nursing program. I hated the whole thing. I was miserable. I would call my mom on the phone and ask her why she was "making me do this." I continued to party, providing myself with no coping skills or self-care practices. Somehow, I made it through. Thirteen months later, I was off to my first job.

A Jekyll and Hyde story

I found myself working on an adult general inpatient psychiatric unit. Coming from my psychology degree, I felt "safest" on a psych unit. And guess what? I actually enjoyed the work—at first.

It was exciting to be a new employee. There was so much to learn, and this was the first time I was collecting a substantial paycheck. I must have been good at my job because I marched up into leadership positions quite quickly. I was giving presentations nationally and internationally, sitting on departmental level committees and chairing committees on my unit. I ran charge nurse on nearly every day shift and was promoted to the highest level of floor nurse possible in less than five years.

Sure, it looked great from the outside. This brand-new nurse was a career success—or, so everyone thought. Inside was a completely different story.

I was a mess. A total wreck. I would come home from work and throw temper tantrums. I was up most nights unable to sleep. I developed digestive issues and fought often with my then-boyfriend.

One night, as I sat breathing heavily after yet another long sobbing session, I "woke up." I realized I couldn't live this way any longer. I was unhappy. I was unhealthy. I hated myself and my life. I decided right then and there that I had to make a change—and quickly.

Light ahead

Once I made my decision that I couldn't live like this anymore, things started to come together.

First, I began to meet with my academic advisor. I was coming to the end of my dual master's degree program, and I thought this would be a great opportunity to find something new using my degree. I also completed a capstone project at a local gym. My group put together the gym's social media platform (this was in 2009, right around the time social media was really starting to take off), and I got to meet many top-level executives at the company. All I kept saying to anyone who would listen (and, most importantly, to myself) was, "I want to work in wellness and prevention. I want to focus on health and well-being. I want something different."

Less than two months after that capstone project was completed and my graduation celebrated, I was offered a job running a physician-referred exercise program at the wellness center! To my delight (and total surprise, as I didn't even dream a job like this was possible), I was given a second chance as a nurse.

Self-care shifted my perspective

At the wellness center, I was not only working with health, but I was surrounded by it. I started to try out the exercise machines myself. Once my body had more energy, I was interested in learning about diet, rest, and mindfulness practices. I enrolled as a student in a coaching program and, after completing the first one, went through a second!

Sure, the physical and emotional healing was wonderful—and needed. But something even more magical happened during that time: my perspective shifted.

Towards the end of my time working on the inpatient psych unit, I was a classic victim. Everything wrong was everyone else's fault: the organization for not taking care of their employees, the unit management for not enforcing the rules equally, my own colleagues for calling out and not working as hard as me. Everyone else was to blame. I hated being a nurse and I couldn't stand to be around anyone.

That all changed when I realized there was only one thing constant and only one person standing at the center of all of this chaos: *me*.

I was the one not taking care of myself. I was the one putting myself in harm's way. I was burned out, not only from my career, but from my life.

Nursing from within

These days, I am singing a completely different tune. In fact, I have gone back and apologized to my mom. I now love being a nurse and am grateful for every single experience in my career.

And the best news? Since having a coach was a huge factor in my 180-degree turnaround, I have become a coach and trainer to nurses. My goal is to help other nurses heal from the suffering of burnout and reconnect with what they love about being a nurse and helping others.

We go into this work with a desire to take care of others. We enter the profession with noble aims. Unfortunately, we give so much we often lose ourselves along the way. Now, I get to work with nurses across the country, helping them reconnect with the nurses within and allowing them to heal so they can fully enjoy the career they were called to do.

Chapter 1

BURNOUT BASICS

*Everything You Need to Understand About Burnout, But Didn't
Know to Ask*

*"It is difficult to get a man to understand something
when his salary depends upon his not understanding it."*
—Upton Sinclair

"If you have always done it that way, it's probably wrong."
—Charles Kettering

WHY IS BURNOUT SUCH A BIG DEAL
FOR NURSES?

Nursing is one of the most difficult professions. Not only is it physically exhausting, but the mental and emotional toll can create havoc in the individual nurse's life. From sleepless nights to raging emotions, burnout can affect the nurse—and everyone with whom he or she interacts.

In healthcare, the effects of nurse burnout have negative—and potentially fatal—repercussions for a huge swath of society. In no other occupation does burnout exact such a toll of waste, morbidity, and mortality.

<u>Nurse burnout has been linked to:</u>

- Poorer mental health
- Job dissatisfaction
- Lower levels of patient satisfaction
- Increased costs related to turnover
- More frequent adverse patient events
- Greater intention to leave the job
- Increased absenteeism
- More frequent medical errors

- Higher levels of emotional exhaustion
- Issues with a nursing shortage[3]

The bottom line is this: nurse burnout sends out huge ripples of pervasively negative effects in all directions.

Burnout is bad:

- For the nurse
- For their family
- For their patients
- For their staff, colleagues, and coworkers
- For their organization

But wait, there's more …

Burnout is everywhere, all the time.

BURNOUT SIGNIFICANCE

The significance of symptomatic burnout is staggeringly high in professional nurses. Consider the following quote from one of the main researchers on nurse staffing, satisfaction, and burnout from an article several years back in the *Journal of the American Medical Association (JAMA)*:

> *Forty percent of hospital nurses have burnout levels that exceed the norms for health care workers. Job dissatisfaction among hospital nurses is 4 times greater than the average for all US workers, and 1 in 5 hospital nurses report that they intend to leave their current jobs within a year.*[4]

In fact, the connection between burnout and job satisfaction is the single most thoroughly studied aspect of this issue. Nurses are repeatedly given the Maslach Burnout Inventory Scale in order to measure this relationship.

As this book goes to press, the acceleration of practice change in the US healthcare market driven by the Affordable Care Act appears to be causing burnout prevalence to reach new highs in many organizations.

And yet, most healthcare workplaces completely fail to acknowledge stress, burnout, and overwhelm. The nursing staff runs on their gerbil wheels as fast as they can. You might finish your shift at seven, give report, work on your documentation until eight, drag yourself home for dinner, put in two hours of homework with the kids at home, only to stagger back into an identical day tomorrow. Sound familiar? It is certainly common. That, however, is not the worst part.

LEADERSHIP FOCUS IS THE BIGGER TRAGEDY

In many organizations, leaders find themselves in a catch-22. They are aware of the high costs related to nurse burnout and subsequent turnover, yet they are often unable to do anything about it. When faced with budgetary cuts, staffing policies, and competing quality indicators, "soft" items such as employee satisfaction and well-being get bumped from the agenda.

Nursing leaders understand the relationship between nurse burnout and turnover. Research has shown that work environments with higher-than-average emotional exhaustion and higher-than-average depersonalization increase the likelihood of a nurse's intention to leave. However, nursing executives struggle with figuring out how to solve this issue of nurse burnout—and sustain it over time.

I find this fascinating, given the nature of services we provide in healthcare. We care for others. Our caring is the basis of the business of healthcare. Our caring is what puts dollars in the organization's coffers and supplies the income that is the business's lifeblood. But who is caring for the nurses?

A LESSON FROM INDUSTRIES OUTSIDE HEALTHCARE

Look at any industry outside of healthcare, and listen to what the acknowledged leaders say about their people. Inevitably, a reporter gets around to asking, "To what do you attribute your company's success?"

The leader will then say something like, "It's simple really. We hire the best people we can find and take really good care of them."

Why does healthcare not follow this rule?

If you find yourself in a hostile workplace where no one seems to understand or care about your personal health or your workplace conditions, I invite you to dive into this book and learn how to look out for yourself. You will learn a number of ways to improve your current situation and how to conduct a high-quality job search if it is healthier for you to move on. You will also learn new ways to ask for what you want inside a bureaucracy and have a much higher chance of success.

If you find yourself in a forward-thinking organization that cares about you and works to provide the support you need to do a good job with your patients, congratulations. It is highly likely they gave you this book. You can use the following tools to focus squarely on creating your Ideal Practice and build a relationship with your leaders that can improve the workplace for everyone.

Always remember, burnout is not normal or inevitable.

Even though burnout is common, it is not normal. Burnout is identifiable, preventable, and treatable. Burnout even has a highest and best use.

You can use your own stress and burnout to create a more Ideal Practice and a more balanced life—much more quickly than you might imagine.

If you are a leader in a healthcare organization, we are entering healthcare's "Age of Engagement." From this point forward, your proactive efforts to lower stress and create a more nurse-friendly workplace will give you a massive competitive advantage over all other organizations that just keep piling more and more on their nurses' backs.

WHAT IS THE DIFFERENCE BETWEEN BURNOUT AND NORMAL STRESS?

STRESS IS COMMON. It's a normal aspect of modern life. It's nearly constant for a nurse on the job. With stress an ever-present condition for every practicing nurse, how can you tell the difference between the "normal" stress of practicing nursing and burnout?

Before we get to that simple answer, let's remember that stress is not always a bad thing. Without an appropriate amount of stress and challenge, the average human lapses into boredom and inactivity. The stress and responsibility of caring for patients is part of the motivation to do your best in every case. The perfectionism it inspires is a good thing for the patient. However, too much of that good thing is bad for the nurse.

So, what is the difference between the normal stresses of the healthcare workplace and the syndrome of burnout? It's really important that you and I get on the same page here in regards to this critical distinction.

Burnout is not about what is happening to you.

The difference between burnout and normal stress is not the nature of the external events that you find stressful. What one person finds to be stressful, a different person would experience as stimulating, exciting, and even fun. Everyone's situation is unique.

Burnout is about whether or not you can cope with the things you find stressful.

The difference between simple stress and burnout is your ability to respond to and recover from the energy drain caused by the things that stress you out.

With normal stress …

… You are able to recover with time off. You are able to maintain "energetic homeostasis." You can recover your energy, enthusiasm, and drive with adequate rest. Your energy may be higher some days and lower on others. You notice the day-to-day fluctuation in your energy levels; however, you don't feel overwhelmed or incapable of recovery from week-to-week.

With burnout …

… You are unable to recover. Your energy enters the pattern of a relentless downward spiral. There comes a time when you notice you are not bouncing back, and you dread heading back into work. In most cases, a person suffering from burnout will eventually say something like, "I'm not sure how much longer I can go on like this."

The only reason burnout rates can hover in the 30 percent range for decades and not destroy the profession of nursing is because we've been work-hardened to tolerate this energetic drain. Let's face it: our training is a gladiator-style survival contest. We are conditioned to be able to cope with burnout better than all but a handful of other service-oriented professions—law enforcement and active duty military come immediately to mind. We will talk much more about this below when we discuss the pathophysiology of burnout.

This high-level overview will make one thing obvious. If you are burned out or headed in that direction, there is something about the stress of your job and the things you do now to recover that is not working.

You are leaking energy and not replenishing it, like a boat with a hole so large that bailing as fast as you can does not keep you from sinking.

This is why a vacation, sabbatical, or retreat will never cure burnout. Simple time away from work will only provide temporary relief. If you don't fundamentally change how you are working by taking different actions, when you return to the workplace after your break, the excess drain begins anew. There is still a hole in your boat.

MEASURING BURNOUT—THE GOLD STANDARD

IN THE 1970s, a researcher at the University of San Francisco named Christina Maslach, along with her partners Susan Jackson and Michael Leiter, constructed what has become the gold standard in measuring occupational burnout. The twenty-two question survey is known as the Maslach Burnout Inventory (MBI).

<u>**The MBI measures the severity of the three main symptoms of burnout:**</u>

1.) Exhaustion

You are extremely tired and unable to recover. Things are either chronically miserable or on the downward spiral trajectory.

2.) Depersonalization

This is an unfeeling or impersonal attitude toward the people you are meant to serve. You will recognize this as the common healthcare symptom of "compassion fatigue."

The nurse becomes cynical or sarcastic about his or her patients. They may blame the patient for contributing to their own personal stress levels. In some cases, the nurse may have fantasies about getting rid of certain patients in creative ways, such as throwing them out the window or even more bizarre and violent visions.

In some healthcare work environments, depersonalization, sarcasm, and cynicism are constant and pervasive. Individuals will continuously blame and complain about patients in the break room and try to normalize it by calling it "healthy venting." Remember this: compassion fatigue is a symptom of burnout. Being cynical and sarcastic about your patients is not normal, and it is never healthy.

Compassion fatigue is actually a dysfunctional psychological defense mechanism. When you are burned out, a piece of you recognizes that some of the energy drain is from your patients. Your cynicism and sarcasm creates a psychological barrier between you and your patients—the source of your energy drain.

However, compassion fatigue only accelerates your downward spiral, because it violates one of healthcare's prime directives: *The patient comes first.* You feel a few seconds of release from bad-mouthing a non-compliant patient at the cost of feeling much worse shortly thereafter.

3.) Lack of Efficacy

This symptom manifests when you begin to doubt the purpose of the work that you do. A nurse at this stage will say something like, "What's the use? I don't know why I keep going. My work isn't really helping anybody or serving any purpose."

Other nurses will begin to doubt the quality of their work or worry about making a clinical mistake and hurting someone because of their exhaustion and obvious compassion fatigue.

Put them all together and the full MBI expression of burnout includes:

- Exhaustion
- Cynicism, sarcasm, and compassion fatigue
- "What's the use?"

In the years since Christina Maslach and her colleagues constructed the MBI, it has become the most widely used inventory for detecting burnout and measuring its severity in healthcare, education, human services, and many other industries.

GENDER DIFFERENCES IN BURNOUT SYMPTOMS

As more and more male nurses have entered the workforce, recent data provides confirmation that there are gender differences in burnout symptoms. Think about this for a moment. I am certain you know some burned-out nurses. In your mind's eye, put the women on one side and the men on the other. What differences in their behavior do you notice?

A recent paper revealed the following information.[5] I bet it backs up your personal observations.

Female-Pattern Burnout

On average, women experience burnout symptoms in the same order as Christina Maslach originally documented them:

1. Exhaustion
2. Cynicism, sarcasm, compassion fatigue
3. "What's the use?"

Male-Pattern Burnout

On average, male burnout follows this pattern:

1. Cynicism, sarcasm, and compassion fatigue
2. Exhaustion
3. "What's the use?" often goes completely missing. It is rare for a male nurse to doubt the meaning or quality of his work.

This leads to the common stereotype of the male nurse in his fifties, chronically burned out, viciously cynical, often disruptive, who continues to soldier on and tells himself, "I am still doing good work."

One more gender difference

Here is one more gender difference I have noticed from working with hundreds of burned-out nurses: once a woman reaches a certain point in her downward spiral, she will usually confide in someone or ask for help.

Most men do not.

I am often asked why this is the case. I think the explanation is simple and based on differences in neuroanatomy and conditioning between the sexes.

Women tend to discuss emotions. They tend to have female friends they confide in. They find it more difficult to tolerate the emotional toll of the battle between compassion fatigue and "the patient comes first."

In the competitive world of the average man, admitting distress is synonymous with weakness or failure.

Men don't ask directions when lost behind the wheel of a car. They don't ask for help when their career is in jeopardy either. They have fewer close friends and tend not to talk about emotional issues. For many men, reaching out for help—or admitting they can't keep going on like this—feels like a final act of capitulation and surrender that takes place long after the average woman has already admitted her burnout to someone else.

WHAT IS THE PATHOPHYSIOLOGY OF BURNOUT?

REMEMBER PATHOPHYSIOLOGY? THE classes we could only take after learning the normal physiology of the various organ systems? It covers all the different ways infections and diseases do the damage that they do. Cancers can hide from the immune system. Cholera turns our intestinal absorption system inside out to do its dirty work. So what, then, might be the pathophysiology of burnout?

Just how does it take the smartest, hardest-working people on the planet and drag them slowly to their knees?

Before I show you the three-part answer to that question, let's get rid of a metaphor that simply doesn't reflect reality: "My batteries just need recharging."

This is not about your batteries

Imagine the Energizer Bunny™. He is marching along, beating his little drum.

What happens to the rabbit when his battery runs out? He stops dead in his tracks. He cannot walk or beat that drum until you install a new battery.

The difference between a battery-powered toy bunny and a nurse is simple…

You have never, ever, ever stopped

You have a personal experience of working far past the point of your batteries being completely dead. You were trained to keep working on empty and below. You never stop. Never.

What would have happened to your career if you had stopped at any time in your training? What would happen to your patients if you stopped at work?

The battery metaphor for the energy of a nurse is inaccurate. Here is a better one.

Your energetic bank accounts

Think about an energetic bank account. It is just like your checking account, except instead of money, it holds your personal store of life energy. It looks like this:

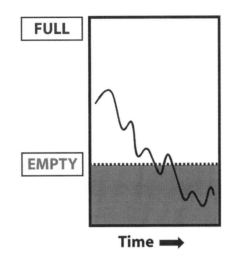

Time ➡

Notice that this energy account has a full mark and an empty mark, but it does not stop at empty. Like most bank accounts, it can fall to a negative balance. You can be below zero and the account still exist.

What happens if you overdraw your checking account? Does the bank close it? Nope. They simply charge you fees and interest, and you go even further into the red. When you cross zero, they simply accelerate your downward spiral.

It is exactly the same for your energy. When you cross the empty boundary, the downward spiral often accelerates. However, you do not stop showing up for work and seeing patients—at least, not for a while.

Here's why: your undergraduate program was a specific, work-hardening process. You were trained to function as a nurse when your energy account was tapped dry. You have been conditioned to run on empty and below.

Studies show you are not at your best when your energy levels are below zero. Your quality of care and patient satisfaction scores will suffer. Despite that, you will still get the work done somehow, finish your shift, and drag your sorry butt home ... right?

Here's the problem: the only way you can do your best work with patients and the only way you can have any reasonable quality of life at home is to somehow maintain a positive balance in your energy account. This brings us to the First Law of Burnout.

THE FIRST LAW OF BURNOUT

"You can't give what you ain't got"

Without a positive balance of personal energy, you have nothing to give. If you continue to put out energy when you are below zero, the care you offer and the life you live will be a shadow of what is possible for you.

Let's go one step further.

Your three energy accounts

Rather than a single energy account, it is very useful to think in terms of three distinct energy accounts. They correspond to each of the three symptoms of the Maslach Burnout Inventory (MBI).

Let me show you each of these three energy accounts in turn and give you a recipe for keeping each of the three accounts in a positive balance.

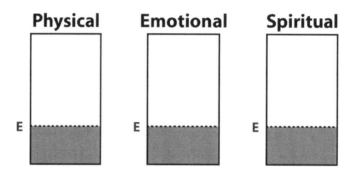

1.) Exhaustion and your physical energy account

The MBI symptom of exhaustion corresponds to an account holding your physical energy. This is a simple enough concept. We are human beings with a physical body to which we must tend. You keep this account full by taking good care of your physical self.

This is another area where our training taught us exactly the opposite. Long shifts, poor nutrition, no exercise, and sleep deprivation are all part of the work-hardening of nursing school. If you have somehow learned how to take good care of yourself, it was not while you were at work.

Each of us must plan and execute a physical care program to keep ourselves healthy. Rest, good food, exercise, and adequate time off for recharge are all important. This is your personal responsibility, no matter what practice structure (from solo to employee) or job situation you find yourself in at the moment.

2.) Compassion fatigue and your emotional energy account

The MBI symptom of cynicism, sarcasm, and compassion fatigue corresponds to an account holding your emotional energy. Remember, "You can't give what you ain't got." If you are not getting your emotional needs met and this account is in a negative balance, you cannot be emotionally present for the pain and suffering of others. This is where compassion fatigue flies in as a defense mechanism and tries to help out by shielding you from continued drain of emotions. Unfortunately, it only makes things worse.

In my experience, you make deposits in your emotional energy account through your important relationships.

Ask yourself this question, "Have I spent an adequate amount of quality time with all the people whom I love and are important to me?" Notice your answer.

Is there someone—a family member, friend, maybe even your significant other—who you owe a phone call, a visit, a cup of coffee, a letter or card? If your answer is yes, write this person's name down and get on it. Make a deposit in your emotional bank account right away.

For most practicing nurses, there is a huge imbalance between the time you spend at work—or after work on work activities—and the time you would like to spend with your children, friends, significant other, and family. How about you?

3.) "What's the use?" And your spiritual energy account

I want to separate the concept of spirituality I am referencing here from any type of religious practice. If you have a religious practice that provides you with joy and meaning, please keep it up.

When I use the word spirituality here, I am talking about your week-to-week connection with a sense of purpose and meaning in your work as a nurse.

In an ideal world, your nursing career would provide you with that sense of purpose and fulfillment early and often. You would have frequent patient interactions where, at the end of the day, you look back and say to yourself, "Oh, yeah, *that* is why I became a nurse!"

This is not to say you must derive your entire sense of purpose from your nursing career. Many of us find our strongest sense of purpose in family activities and other interests outside of nursing.

What provides you with that deep down "oh, yeah" feeling?

You make a deposit into your spiritual energy account whenever you feel that connection between what you are doing and your purpose, when what you are doing feels like *what you are meant to be doing* in this lifetime. You are making the difference you were put here to make with the people you are meant to help.

How—specifically—can you make deposits in your spiritual energy account?

That depends on where you derive your sense of purpose. If we focus only on your nursing career for a moment, let me show you a way to get started.

Grab a piece of paper and a pen. Go on, do it. It does you no good whatsoever to simply read about this exercise.

Write down, in as much detail as you can, your last ideal patient encounter. Write down that last patient visit where you said, "Oh, yeah, that's why I do what I do," or where you came home that evening and shouted out as you walked through the door, "Honey, honey … sit down for a minute, and let me tell you what happened at work today."

Write it down now with all the details you can muster.

- What happened?
- How did it feel?
- Why did it feel that way?

When you are done, read it back to yourself.

- What are the themes you see in this story?
- Is this a particular type of patient or diagnosis or procedure you really like?
- Was it more about the problem or more about your relationship with the patient?
- What else was special about this particular encounter?

And here is the payoff question:

How can you structure your day so this kind of encounter is more frequent?

Setting yourself up to have more frequent ideal patient encounters is an important part of building your Ideal Nursing Career. You can structure your weeks to increase the likelihood of this kind of interaction.

Your spiritual energy account and the triple whammy

Here is a special attribute I have noticed about this third energy account. Check it out and see if this is true for you.

Remember back to your ideal patient encounter—how was your energy for the rest of your day?

Was it lower or higher? How was your physical and your emotional energy later in that shift? Most nurses tell me that as an ideal patient encounter makes a deposit in your spiritual bank account, you can feel the other two energy accounts go up at the same time.

One experience of being connected with your purpose gives you an energy deposit in all three accounts.

It is a true triple whammy.

Remember too, that this same connection with your purpose could come from outside your nursing career. You could get the same triple deposit from coaching your children's soccer team, volunteering to teach kids to read, overseas medical missions, or anything else that feeds your spirit. You can structure your life to increase the frequency of these experiences too.

It is part of stepping off those rails and living with purpose.

Unfortunately, we tend to lose sight of purpose when we are overwhelmed and exhausted. Maintaining your ability to focus on what you love about your practice—and your sense of purpose in what you do—is one of the lessons I hope you take from this book.

Burnout pathophysiology ACTION STEPS

You have been exquisitely trained to ignore your energy levels. Your action step here is simply to notice your own energy balances right now. Using the diagrams below, place an "X" where you feel your energy balances are for your three energy accounts at the moment.

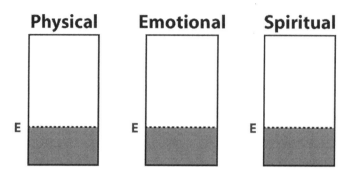

Just becoming aware of your balances in these energy accounts is a huge change for most nurses. Remember, our "patient comes first" training taught us how to completely ignore these energetic signals. It is high time for you to develop the ability to monitor your own energy stores.

Keep in mind: *you can't give what you ain't got.*

What if your energy levels are in the red?

That is OK. Whether your energy levels are positive or negative is not important now. Just notice where you are for now. It is only when you acknowledge your actual energy levels that you can begin to make changes if necessary.

One of my favorite awareness quotes says it all:"The beginning of all change is calling things by their right name."

What are your energy levels?

WHAT ARE THE ROOT CAUSES OF BURNOUT?

WHEN I FIRST started working with nurses, I thought this question had a simple answer. I thought of it like a third-grade math equation.

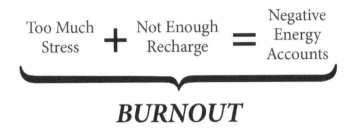

Too much stress on the job and not enough recharge off the job causes a negative energy balance. This situation is the very definition of burnout.

Since then, I have learned the sources of stress and the blockages to recharge are much more complicated than simple third-grade math. Otherwise, why would one-third of our best and brightest be stuck in burnout every day? It is a conundrum for sure.

In my work with overstressed nurses, I have noticed several distinct sources of energy drain that are, in fact, the five main causes of burnout. Some of them are indeed stress-related. Others are the result of blind spots instilled by the conditioning (or, you could say, brainwashing) process of our nursing education.

Let's go through each one. I encourage you to notice that your training only prepared you for one of these five main causes of burnout. No wonder burnout is capable of sneaking up on so many of us.

THE FIVE ROOT CAUSES OF BURNOUT

Burnout Cause #1: the profession—the stress of the clinical practice of nursing

By any measure, healthcare is stressful. Apart from law enforcement and active-duty military (two careers that also have very high burnout rates), practicing nursing may be the most stressful career you could choose.

You have ultimate responsibility and little control over the outcome, but that is not all. The following story will illustrate a little-appreciated stress of being a nurse that all of us notice in our training when we first start seeing live patients. It doesn't take long, though, for this source of stress to fall into a deep blind spot in our awareness.

Talking about this stress to nurses is very much like talking to a fish about the water in its bowl. The fish is completely unaware of the water it swims in.

Everyone who is not in nursing sees this built-in stress of working as a nurse immediately. It becomes invisible for nurses early in our education because it is part of the fabric of every single patient encounter. Let me tell you a little story to illustrate this point.

The party planner vs. the nurse

I have a friend who is a party planner. She owns a business that helps people create, plan, and pull off the most amazing events. When you go to her office, the conversation focuses on dinner menus, color palettes, and fabulous locations.

That is how my friend makes a living. Every time I see her, she is glowing. One afternoon, I asked her what it's like to have this for a job.

She said, "Elizabeth, I love my job. Everyone comes to me for a celebration. It's so much fun; it almost never feels like work to me!"

Think about that for a second. How is being a nurse different than owning a party planning business—or almost any other job?

No one wants to come and see you ... ever.

They don't expect to have a good time during their visit to the clinic under most circumstances. Even a routine physical is filled with trepidation. The patients are not sure what they might find out.

Even if the person is not the patient and is simply a family member visiting in the hospital or accompanying the patient on a clinic visit, you're the face of the medical profession to them. You personify the health issues facing their loved ones.

Our "clients" are sick, hurting, injured, scared, suffering, and sometimes in the very act of dying. Every visit is veiled by a mist of these negative emotions. You can't escape this reality. It quickly fades from our awareness. It never actually goes away.

For all the reasons mentioned above—and many more you will learn in the pages that follow—the modern environment of healthcare is stressful.

Even if I could magically shift you from room to room in a Star Trek-like transporter beam and relieve you of all documentation requirements (wouldn't that be nice!), allowing you the classic nurse's dream experience of "just caring for patients"—

even that day would leave you drained. You can't care for patients and somehow avoid putting energy into your day.

And then there are the bad days

No one can make it through nursing school and out onto the floor without being traumatized by horrific events along the way. We all have stories we have never told anyone. We have all seen things happen we wish we hadn't. It goes with the territory. Each of us has one or more traumatic experiences from our past that is capable of blowing a "normal" day to pieces when circumstances align themselves to remind us of the original incident.

Each of us also knows that every patient could be the next medication error or call to the rapid-response team.

This work is stressful in so many ways.

The energetic reality

From the standpoint of your energy accounts, you cannot work as a nurse without expending physical, emotional, and spiritual energy. You will come home with less energy than when you arrived at the beginning of your shift.

... And the exception

The one exception is if you had a major ideal patient encounter that day and created your own triple-whammy energy deposit. For most nurses, these types of encounters are rare and their career is not designed to deliver them with any frequency.

It is very important to note that this is the only burnout cause you had any experience with when you graduated from nursing school. You will soon see you are completely unprepared for the remaining four burnout causes. Hang on to your hat.

Burnout Cause #2: your specific job

The second root cause of burnout is the stress associated with *your specific job position*. These stresses are deposited in an additional layer on top of the level one stresses of the practice of clinical medicine outlined above.

A very incomplete list of job-specific stresses includes:

- Your rotating schedule and on-call shifts

- The Electronic Medical Record in your institution, the IT capabilities that support the EMR, and your specific documentation requirements—including the regulations governing how you document, such as medication orders, pain protocols, and others
- Your support staff and your relationships and delegation abilities in leading your team
- Your holiday schedule and weekend hours
- Your relationships with nurse colleagues and administrative leadership
- The expectation for you to participate in activities viewed as professional development, such as committee work, evidence-based research, and specialty certifications, which you are typically not compensated for
- Your confidence in your team's abilities to adequately care for your patients when you leave your shift
- The uncertainty and threat of overwhelming patient volumes brought into play by the Affordable Care Act (Obamacare) and the shift from volume to value in the US

And on and on and on it goes. Add any remaining stresses you are feeling in your current job to the end of this large list.

These additional job-associated stresses can make pulling the curtain shut—and having your seven-and-a-half minutes with the patient—an island of sanity in what feels like a crazy career choice.

These stresses hit below the belt as well. The only way to deal with them effectively is to use skill sets you were never taught.

Your missing skill sets

Nursing school trains you to be a competent clinician. Within your specialty, you are experienced in assessing a patient, creating and implementing a plan, and then evaluating progress towards goals. Unfortunately, that is not enough to build your ideal career.

Now that you are a working nurse, your job responsibilities could really use several additional skill sets. There was no room in nursing school to teach you these, and they would really come in handy now. Here is a partial list:

- Leadership
- Project management

- Business development
- Business finance
- Team communication

(To name a few.)

When you add these job specific stresses to the stress of just caring for patients, your workday can quickly force you into survival mode. We will go into survival mode in full detail in the next chapter. It is vital that you be able to recognize this early symptom of burnout.

Job-related stresses differ by specialty and location.

The stresses you experience from your job are often determined by the where and how of your specific nursing job choice. Job-related stress is universal; the "flavor" of the stress is different depending on whether your nursing career is:

- Hospital-Based
  - Clinical Staff
  - Advanced Practice Role
  - Director/Executive Level Leadership
- Long-Term Care Facility
  - Adult Day Services
  - Assisted Living
  - Rehabilitation Centers
  - Hospice Care
  - Nursing Homes
- Academic
  - Nursing Research
  - Joint Faculty
  - Professor of Nursing

The list goes on and on. You can see this is not a comprehensive list of all of the different roles nurses fill by any means.

Then there's the stress of working inside a bureaucracy. The more people you interact with on a daily basis, the more your stress levels can increase as you navigate the chain of command and different silo mentalities that inevitably form.

Beware of magical thinking

You may be tempted to think changing your job or your nursing specialty will eliminate all your stress. You hear this when a nurse says something like, "If I left the hospital setting …" or, "If I just become a nurse educator, everything will be so much easier."

This is a form of magical thinking. Every job position and each nursing specialty has its own unique set of stressors.

If you do change jobs or nursing specialties, the change rarely brings the stress relief you seek. You simply trade one flavor of stress for another. Often, I meet nurses at the point where they have done exactly this: jumped from the frying pan into the fire. This happens because you changed jobs or specialties because you were running away from your last job. To create your ideal career, you must know what you would run towards. Much more in Chapter 3.

Burnout Cause #3: having a life

For most nurses, your larger life is the place where you recharge. You rest and recuperate and make deposits in your energy accounts when you are off the job.

There is a huge assumption here though. We all assume you know *how* to recharge when you are not at work. We both know it is not a skill you were ever actually taught. Sure, you would come home from a long shift as a nursing student, grab whatever you could to eat, and crash until the next day. But that is not true recharge or authentic life balance.

The 800-pound gorilla

Left to its own devices, your career is very much like living with a wild 800-pound silverback gorilla.

Imagine you live with a wild gorilla in your house right now. How much room would that gorilla leave you … in your own house? Where would he poop?

Imagine now that the gorilla is your career choice to be a nurse and the house is your life. Left to its own devices, your career can take up all the room in your life and make a mess whenever and wherever it wants.

The gorilla-that-is-your-career can completely dominate your personal time and all your major relationships. It can feel like you only get the cold leftovers to yourself. If it feels that way to you, I wonder how it feels to your spouse or significant other?

You have never been taught the skills to create and maintain life balance. You have to learn them on your own, by trial and error, all while simultaneously balancing the stresses of a nursing career and your specific job.

And life has a tendency to get more complicated as we get older.

Occasionally, nursing students will marry and start a family before they graduate. However, most of us begin that phase in our lives after taking our first job position. This is usually a huge time and energy demand we never needed to add into the mix and cope with until now.

Whether you are single, married, in relationship or not, have one child or six or none, your larger life has many ways to add additional stress to the stresses of your nursing career and your job.

More examples:

- Your relationship with your spouse or significant other
- Children and raising and caring for a family
- Your own physical health and fitness
- Finances (saving money, paying off debt, investments, etc.)
- Your wider family responsibilities, including caring for aging parents, etc.
- Hobbies, friendships, and interests outside of nursing

Most of us are able to grow a life and find some balance by trial and error. We learn to get some exercise and sleep and deal with the additional time commitments of our lives outside of healthcare. Our skill in this balancing act varies from week to week, and everyone is on their own to figure it out.

What if things don't go well?

If anything happening outside of work begins to block your ability to recharge your energy accounts, you are in trouble. These blocks to recharge at home can actually be a cause of burnout at work.

If you are a nurse leader, it is important to understand this. High stress levels at home can prevent recharge. This will show up as burnout on the job, even when the problem is not on the job site at all.

Let me emphasize this point. If someone looks for all the world like they are entering the downward spiral of burnout at work … *it may have nothing to do with work.*

If you are a manager checking in with a colleague who seems to be struggling, make sure you ask, "How are things going at home?"

You won't uncover these life-based issues unless you ask. Here is a partial list of possibilities:

- Conflict in the nurse's primary relationship, including separation and divorce
- Birth of a child, third child, twins
- Problems with children—from special needs to behavior issues and more
- Financial hardships
- Personal health issues
- Wider family issues such as the failing health of a parent

If you have these additional stressors in your life, it is vitally important to continue to take good care of yourself, despite the extra stress and responsibility at home. The first law of burnout applies here too. When it comes to successfully navigating these life stresses, "You can't give what you ain't got."

In some cases, you will need to cut back on work responsibilities to have the time and energy to deal with these issues in your life outside of nursing.

Burnout Cause #4: the leadership skills of your immediate supervisor

Outside of the healthcare industry, there is a widely accepted mantra that goes like this: "People don't quit the company; they quit their boss."

If you think back to your own personal work experience—both as a nurse and before you started nursing—you will see this is probably true for you too. Nearly everyone has had the experience of quitting a good job because of a bad boss. The work was pretty good, but the hostility or ineffectiveness of your boss was what drove you out of that job.

Since most nurses are in an employee role, this means your boss has a massive influence on your stress levels at work and your quality of life itself. The stress that comes from a bad or missing boss functions independently from the remaining four causes of burnout.

You can love your work and your life and recognize all your programming (see below), and still be driven from your job by a terrible boss.

This topic is so important that we have dedicated a full section of this book to the skills of Managing Your Boss. Look for it in Chapter 5, where we will also show you how to radically upgrade your own leadership skills.

Burnout Cause #5: the conditioning of our nursing education

When I first started working with burned-out nurses, I often ran into mysterious brick walls. I would point out something obvious they were doing to make themselves miserable, and it appeared they were incapable of seeing what I was seeing. It was talking to a fish about water again.

It became clear over time that nurses have a network of blind spots in their awareness. There are a set of things about being a nurse they can't see that they can't see. I saw these issues clearly from the outside, but only because I had been out of the day-to-day of floor nursing for several years.

The general public sees these unique features of being a nurse quite clearly. Often, they think this is just how nurses are. You can hear it in their language: "Nurses care for everyone but themselves" or other similar pronouncements.

From my perspective, it is clear that nurses are not born this way. I believe there is no such thing as a typical nurse personality. The people underneath the RN are always unique and as varied as any segment of the normal population.

Yet, as nurses, we are actually conditioned to think and act in a very similar fashion from nurse to nurse.

Nursing education is a conditioning process

We are taught to play the role of nurse in a very specific and standardized way. It was only when I recognized I was witnessing true conditioning—brainwashing, if you will—that I was able to fundamentally change the way I approached my career as a nurse. Understanding that subconscious conditioning is often driving your behavior —ambushing you from a blind spot in your awareness— will help you see this cause of burnout.

In my experience, this is often the most important of the five causes of burnout in a nurse. The paragraphs below will outline this conditioning in full detail.

Remember too, that this is subconscious. These are things you can't see that you can't see. Things you don't know you don't know. They sit in blind spots created by your nursing education. I encourage you to read the following section at least three times or consider reading it with your significant other or a good friend to bring your conditioning fully into the light of day.

Five flavors of nurse conditioning

Here are the five major "flavors" of conditioning I see in nurses. There are many more minor aspects of conditioning nurses exhibit, but these are the big five that most commonly get in the way of our happiness.

1. Workaholic
2. Superhero
3. Emotion-free
4. Lone Ranger
5. Perfectionist

Before they became subconscious conditioning, we learned each of these as distinct and very useful skill sets. Let's face it—there were hundreds of times in your nursing education the skills of a workaholic or a perfectionist or a person who is capable of being emotion-free came in handy. In fact, you could not have become a nurse without them.

In an ideal world, you would have been taught to use them the way a carpenter uses the tools on his belt. You pull out a hammer when it is the best tool for the job at hand. You use it to drive in that nail, and then you slide it back into the loop on your tool belt where it belongs. When you are done with your power tool, you turn it off and put it away.

When you are done with work, you take your tool belt off and put it away until your next day on the job.

Those are healthy boundaries.

Early in our education, we hone and practice these skill sets constantly. We become experts in their use, even as undergrads. We need them just to survive the training process of nursing school and then residency.

Here is one of the differences between a nurse and a carpenter:

No one ever showed you how to turn your tools off and put them away.

We have no tool belt we can simply unclip and hang on a hook when we get home.

Very early in our education, we actually become our tools.

We become workaholic, superhero, emotion-free, Lone Ranger perfectionists. Without knowing how to turn them off and put them away, we start to live our whole lives this way. People outside of nursing look at nurses and think, *that's just the way nurses are.* What they are really seeing is this deep, comprehensive, and subconscious conditioning. This is one of the prices we pay to survive the education process. It sets us up for burnout down the road.

Recognizing your programming

- Recognize your workaholic programming when your only solution to any problem is to work harder, and you get angry at people who don't work as hard as you.
- Recognize the superhero programming when you feel you should save everyone or get very upset when you can't.
- Recognize your emotion-free programming is in play when you notice you have feelings about a specific patient—and immediately feel guilty or inadequate for not being the perfect emotion-free and detached clinician.
- Recognize the Lone Ranger programming when you are stuck in the maze of doing everything yourself, despite having a team around you.
- Recognize the perfectionist programming when you agonize over details that are not clinically relevant, or chastise patients and your staff for minor imperfections.

If you happen to be an overstressed and burned-out nurse, this programming actively gets in your way when you are trying to turn the downward spiral around. One of the keys to your recovery is recognizing the difference between your voice and the voices of these programmed pieces of your nurse persona.

But, wait. There's more.

The nurse's two prime directives

In addition to the five main "flavors" of programming listed above, we are deeply conditioned to operate by two prime directives.

Prime Directive #1: *"The patient comes first."*

This mantra sets up a pecking order. Patient first ... me somewhere down the line. This is in direct conflict with the first law of burnout: *you can't give what you ain't got.*

Your ability to care for a patient is completely dependent upon maintaining a positive balance in your energy accounts. The patient simply cannot always come first. You must have time where you put yourself first in order to recharge. This makes the same sense as third-grade math, but this basic truth seems to be hidden in most healthcare workplaces.

This prime directive is a direct block to recharging.

If you operate by the principle of *the patient comes first* at all times, this mindset is a major cause of your stress and burnout. It is the source of your guilty feelings when you actually block out time for yourself and do something "selfish" like read a book or take a nap in your time away from work.

The thought that this activity is selfish comes from your workaholic programming. You see that, yes?

If you look at other professions that put their "client" first, you will have a who's who of the highest burnout industries. A partial list includes hotel, restaurant, and other hospitality categories, counselors and teachers, healthcare, law enforcement, and active-duty military.

The patient comes first is a recipe for burnout if there is no off switch or protected space from its command.

Prime Directive #2: *"Never show weakness."*

If you have any doubt this is true for nurses, consider this scenario:

Remember back when you were a new grad. Imagine your charge nurse coming to you and asking, "Hey, how are you doing? You look beat. Do you need any help?" What would you have said in return? Be honest.

We both know the answer to that question. It would go something like this:

"What? I'm fine. Don't need a thing. Couldn't be better. A break? No—I've got an admission from the ED. I can eat later. I'm good." Or something along those lines.

Our education is a gladiator-style survival process. The last one standing is seen as the "good nurse." If you show signs that you "can't take it," you are shuffled off to the side and avoided like a leper.

This conditioning never goes away. It actively blocks our ability to recognize when we are not okay. It completely blocks our ability to ask for help, no matter how far into the downward spiral of burnout we may be. I personally believe it is part of the reason nurse turnover rates are as high as they are and growing exponentially.

Realize no one actually tried to do this to you on purpose.

There is no one to blame here. It is important to note that despite the power and the comprehensive nature of the conditioning of our education, no one tried to do this to you on purpose. The faculty in your nursing school did not plot to instill these blind spots in the break room while you were out on the units. The forces that condition nurses are woven into the fabric of the experience of your education going back generations.

The power of this conditioning is immense.

The key to the depth of our brainwashing is the intensity and length of the education process we use to produce a nurse.

Do you know anything about basic training in the military? It lasts six to twelve weeks, depending on the branch of service. We all know basic training is a conditioning process, right? By the time that brief, but intense, process is through, an eighteen-year-old recruit will walk into a live-fire exercise when asked to do so. The only reason they follow that insane request is because their conditioning now sees that as an "order" they must obey.

Minus the deadly weapons, do you think nursing school was any less intense than military training? Add up the years between your first day of your nursing education and the day you became a nurse. How long was that for you?

Do you think it is possible you were conditioned just a tiny little bit in that time?

SUMMARY OF THE CAUSES OF BURNOUT

1.) The Profession: The stress of the clinical practice of nursing.

2.) The Job: The stresses of your specific job position that are independent of the stress of caring for patients.

3.) Having a Life: The stress of maintaining your physical health, building and maintaining life balance, and the ability to recharge your energy accounts when you are not at work.

4.) The Leadership Skills of Your Immediate Supervisor: The stress of having a bad boss or no boss at all.

5.) The Programming of Our Nursing Education:

- Workaholic—Superhero—Emotion-Free—Lone Ranger—Perfectionist
- "The patient comes first"
- "Never show weakness"

Your new awareness can make a big difference

Simply being aware of this programming will help you notice the habits it has created. I hope you can also see how your nursing education did not teach you about four of these five causes of burnout. Unfortunately, most nurses don't learn about burnout until after they are suffering from it. Now, you are fully informed and will be able to see the causes of burnout in real time as you notice them in the days, weeks, and years ahead.

Share this knowledge

I strongly encourage you to share this chapter with your spouse or significant other. Remember, much of this lies hidden in your blind spots. Your spouse or significant other is your early warning system for burnout behavior when you are in survival mode and revert to pure programming.

Causes of burnout ACTION STEPS

Grab your journal, a nice pen, and your favorite beverage, and dive into the exercises below.

1.) The Profession of Nursing:
- Make a list of the things that stress you about being a nurse … things that are an unavoidable part of being a nurse in the first place.
- How can you acknowledge these things are stressful and prepare for them or recharge from them more effectively?

2.) Your Job:
- What things stress you about your current job position and its responsibilities … things that would change if you changed jobs?
- What might you do to delegate, redesign, prepare for them, or recharge more effectively?

3.) Having a Life:
- What are your favorite activities to recharge when you are off work?
- What things are going on in your life right now that make it difficult to recharge at home?
- What might you do differently to amplify your ability to recharge and avoid some of the stresses taking place in your larger life away from work?

4.) The Leadership Skills of Your Immediate Supervisor:
- What are your favorite qualities of your immediate supervisor?
- What would you like them to start doing / stop doing / keep doing?
- When will you meet with them to work on building trust and your working relationship? (See the section below on How to Manage Your Boss for a number of suggestions for that meeting.)

5.) The Programming of Your Nursing Education:

Let's restore some balance to the Force here. Try this exercise to reveal some of the programming you absorbed since the day you started nursing school. This will help you begin letting go of the pieces of the programming that are not healthy.

I encourage you to read the following statements and contemplate on, journal about, and even discuss them with your colleagues.

- It is okay—in fact, it is absolutely necessary—to take care of my personal needs for sleep, nutrition, exercise, and time with the people I love. This is not being selfish. I don't need to feel guilty. I must recharge for one simple reason: *you can't give what you ain't got.*
- It is okay—normal, in fact—to have times when I am down, struggling, trashed, and need a break. At those times, it is okay to tell someone and ask for help and support. I am not being weak, selfish, a wimp, or in a situation of not being able to take it.
- It is okay to delegate tasks to my team, especially when I am not the most qualified person for the task at hand. I don't have to—and simply can't—do it all myself.
- There are many places in life where good enough is good enough. I don't always have to be perfect. Instead of always being perfect, I can ask myself, *Is perfection necessary here?* If not, I can take a breath and let it go.
- The patient cannot always come first. That is insane. It is a recipe for burnout. I can learn how to create a boundary between work and home and create time when family and I come first.
- I don't have to have all the answers. I can lead by asking questions and tap the power of my patients, their families, and my larger team.
- It is impossible to avoid feeling emotions when I am taking care of my patients. To be emotion-free is incompatible with caring. I know I will have emotions, and I know it is okay to feel them. I can learn how to feel and not be drained or weakened by my feelings.

WHAT DOES THE EXPERIENCE OF BURNOUT FEEL LIKE?

"Burnout ... an erosion of the soul caused by a deterioration of one's values, dignity, spirit, and will."
—Christina Maslach

WHEN WE TALK about the symptoms of burnout, we are in a third-person perspective. It is like talking about the symptoms of a heart attack when you are observing another person having one. This is the normal perspective of a professional nurse. You are helping other people understand and treat their symptoms. Being a nurse is not about you and your symptoms.

Then, there's burnout.

You must be able to recognize the primary experience for yourself and understand what to do about it. Now, I do not recommend you try to diagnose and treat your own chest pain; however, I do recommend you be on the lookout for burnout at all times. It is one of the few times you must self-diagnose or listen carefully to your spouse or significant other. Recognizing your own burnout as it is happening is another missing skill set from nursing school, and one of the primary reasons I wrote this book.

Let's talk about what it feels like to experience burnout from a first-person perspective—not a scholarly discussion of symptoms, but what you are thinking and feeling when you look in the mirror in the morning, your energy accounts tapped dry, dreading another day on the unit.

Survival mode

When your energy accounts drop below zero, your subconscious silently switches into survival mode. You can tell this by noticing the following thought pattern: *I just want to get through the day.*

You know you are in survival mode when you look at today's schedule and can think of only one thing: *How can I make it to the end of this shift as quickly as possible and get out of here?* Another common feeling is to dread going in to work in the first place.

In survival mode, you will tend to be upset with anything or anyone who presents a complication, hassle, or interruption to getting the work done. These frustrations will sneak out of your mouth in the form of cynicism or sarcasm and other verbal signs of compassion fatigue.

Your staff, patients, and family may see it as a stiffening of your posture when the charge nurse tells you, "Nurse Sue just called, and she's not coming into work. Someone's going to have to stay late today," or something similar.

Inside, you may or may not recognize frustration, extreme fatigue, anger (to the point of fury), hopelessness, and a whole host of negative emotions.

Your physiology and subconscious thought processes are focused purely on survival.

They see your work as the source of an energy drain that is threatening your integrity as a living organism. They are shutting down your higher functions so you can still function as a nurse in a state of minimal energy outflow.

When you are at home, you may find it very difficult to shut off your thoughts about your job. This is especially true if you are a newer nurse and worry if you did everything right on your shift. Or if you have not learned how to disconnect yourself from frustration about the coworker who is always late.

In survival mode, you may notice a little voice in your head saying things like:

> *I'm not sure how much longer I can go on like this.*
> *I don't understand what is happening here. I keep working harder and harder, but it's like I can't ever catch up.*
> *This is crazy. This is not what I thought my career would be like.*
> *Am I crazy? Is something wrong with me?*
> *If this keeps going, I'm afraid I am going to make a mistake and someone will get hurt.*

Your significant other and other family members may notice your exhaustion and dissatisfaction and comment on it. They may have been commenting on your stress for years now. You will most likely attempt to soldier on or figure it out for yourself. You were trained to respond in this way. This is workaholic, superhero, Lone Ranger, "never show weakness" programming at its finest.

In some cases, your colleagues or the administrators of your group may talk to you about your energy and attitude. This occurs most often when your burnout leads to outbursts of what they see as disruptive behavior. The complaints about your words or actions can come from staff members, colleagues, or patients. Typically, you feel bad about the incidents, yet justify what you did or said as a reasonable response given the situation.

Taking time off cannot reverse burnout

Here is a lesson I learned the hard way and a common mistake many nurses make. You take a break, thinking you just need to "recharge your batteries," and you are right back in survival mode within hours to days of returning to work. If you remember the pathophysiology of burnout, you now understand what happened. When you understand the energy account mechanism of burnout, you know taking a break only provides a short break from burnout.

Whether you take a long weekend, an extended vacation, or go to a conference or retreat in an effort to recharge those batteries, you will find your energy is only temporarily improved. It cannot be any other way. To remain in a positive balance in your energy accounts, you must change the actions that drained you in the first place. Lower your stress levels, increase your ability to recharge, or both.

Without significant changes in your actions, your energy accounts may bounce back above zero (assuming you know how to recharge in the time you take off), but when you return to work, what does your energy do? Yes, it will eventually fall back below zero again.

The natural history of burnout

There are several directions burnout can take once it sets in:

1. You can recognize it and change your actions, habits, routines, and your relationship with your career to recover.
2. It can become a chronic condition, often accompanied by disruptive behavior.
3. You can suffer a complication such as alcohol or other substance abuse, divorce, depression, or suicide.
4. You can quit making a living as a nurse by either changing careers or retiring.

The rest of this book will focus on option one above: recognize and recover. Before I show you several ways to get your energy accounts into a positive balance, though, I encourage you to aim higher than just treating or preventing burnout.

Let me show you how to put burnout to its highest and best use.

The experience of burnout ACTION STEPS

Get out your journal and invest some time with these questions

- How do you know when you are in survival mode?
- Tell your significant other, a good friend, or your children about burnout and survival mode and ask them how *they can tell when you are in it.*
- When your energy is tapped out, what is the favorite phrase of the little voice in *your* head?

WHAT IS BURNOUT'S HIGHEST AND BEST USE?

"It's better to burn out
than to fade away."
—Neil Young

"At every single moment of one's life,
one is what one is going to be
no less than what one has been."
—Oscar Wilde

FROM WITHIN THE misery of nurse burnout, it is difficult to see the possibility of a purpose to this suffering. Let me reassure you, though, that burnout actually has a highest and best use. When you do a good job of recovering from burnout, you will look back on this as the point when everything turned for the better. Rather than fight burnout or fall victim to it, you can use it to stop the downward spiral, creating a new and better reality for yourself and your family in the process.

Here's how I know this: I have worked with hundreds of burned-out nurses at this point, and a clear and universal pattern has emerged. Let me show it to you.

Try this snippet of anthropologic research

Think of a nurse you respect and look up to, someone you feel has his or her act together in work and private life. Ask if you can have a cup of coffee and a conversation. When you are together, I encourage you to make this request:

"Please, tell me your burnout story."

The more you look up to this person—the cooler you think they are—the more likely they are to respond by saying, "Which one?"

I encourage you to listen to the story you are told. It will be of a turning point where this person finally stepped away from a situation that was not working. The story often ends with something like, "… and thank God that happened, or I would still be back in that grind and none of this would be possible."

Burnout marks the normal transitions of life

Here is my experience after listening to nurses in all specialties: the lifetime incidence of nurse burnout is right around 200 percent.

It seems that people don't often get their act together without burnout. Burnout marks the place where you have followed someone else's path long enough that your body is telling you things must change in ways you can no longer ignore. You finally pull your head up and realize beyond any doubt that this is not your path.

If you continue on this route, you will violate your own values, deny the people you love, and most likely slide into a "life of quiet desperation." Burnout gets you to finally say, "I can't do this anymore. There has to be another way."

Unless you turn the downward spiral around before this crisis point, nurse burnout will eventually push you to near breaking. I hope and pray that when you reach that point, you bend and spring back rather than snap like some of the unfortunate among our brothers and sisters. Alcohol, drugs, depression, other mental illnesses, and suicide are all complications I hope you avoid. The good news is that only a tiny minority of nurses will face those trials.

The rest of us are left with a scene Robert Frost described best. You can see that there is more than one option available. It is clear you are free to choose between the two. Either choice has its own set of unique consequences.

> *Two roads diverged in a wood that day and I,*
> *I took the one less traveled by*
> *And that has made all the difference.*
> —Robert Frost

At this point, when you have no energy left to keep putting out the fires of other people's demands and priorities, something important happens. You realize with undeniable clarity that you have other choices available, and the path you have been on all this time is simply one choice among many.

Then, reality hits you like a brick wall.

1.) You can keep fighting all the things that you don't want. You can keep trying to fix the problems by working harder.
Or,
2.) You can decide what you really want in your career, your life, and your relationships with the people you love. You can get crystal clear on that instead … and go get it.

> *No matter how far you have gone on a wrong road, turn back.*
> —Turkish proverb

The train on someone else's tracks

It is as if you became a little train engine on your first day of nursing school and climbed onto a set of tracks someone else had laid down. The tracks led in a straight line to your nursing degree. The only way off was to derail yourself. Each of us remembers one person who fell off the rails of nursing school, but that was not you.

As a new graduate, you moved to a new set of tracks that led you to full-fledged independent nurse. There was no wiggle room. If you played the game by the specialty rules, you ended up progressing forward to certification and possibly an advanced degree.

In your job, you switched to another set of tracks. These are the rails of "the way we do things around here." These are still not your tracks. You did not lay them. However, just like a good nursing student, you chugged down the tracks until it became clear they were headed in a direction that didn't give you the fulfillment and life balance you dreamed of in your education. It was supposed to be different once you passed the NCLEX … right? Here's what you missed.

You didn't realize that you don't have to run on anyone else's tracks anymore. You have the skills and ability to take your career in a number of directions now. You can design and implement your career and your larger life from now on. Honest.

Burnout is when you figure out how to lay your own tracks, or, better yet, realize you are a four-wheel-drive vehicle—not a train confined to its tracks. You can navigate any terrain you choose. The way you have been doing things up until now is only one of the options available.

Burnout is hard-wired into nurses

Much of the struggle and ultimate crisis of nurse burnout is rooted in human neuroanatomy and the conditioning of our nursing education.

We are creatures of habit. Most of our habits as practicing nurses were instilled deep in our subconscious by the nursing education process. And we cannot deny that our human wiring and gender play a role.

- We are wired deep in the reticular activating system to be on the lookout for and avoid pain and danger. The two basic animal instincts are to move toward pleasure and away from pain. The avoidance of pain is a much stronger impulse. It is a foundational feature of our human behavior and neuroanatomy.
- Our nursing education teaches us to see danger everywhere. Everyone is sick until proven otherwise. Each patient encounter offers the opportunity for a

missed medication and disaster. Our fear of professional failure raises catastro-
phizing and paranoia to an art form.

- We are conditioned as new graduate nurses to be workaholic, superhero, emotion-free, Lone Ranger perfectionists. No one shows us the off switch.
- Since the first day of nursing school, we have been 100 percent focused on doing what other people want us to do. Despite exhaustion, sleep deprivation,
burnout, come hell or high water, we get the job done, because the patient
comes first, dammit.

With this as a backdrop, we face all challenges, problems, issues, and concerns
in our lives in the same way. We work harder in an attempt to bulldoze the problem
with sheer will and massive effort.

Good luck with that. It is an old habit pattern. It won't work with everything. It
won't give you any quality of life. Your significant other won't love you more for this
tendency of yours.

Then nurse burnout wears you down to a nub

Your ability to continue on these tracks and this path falls away. You really can't go
on like this for much longer.

Here is where meaningful change can start. It can come in the form of a full-blown,
crash-and-burn crisis or by a simple conscious choice to start doing things differently.
I sincerely hope you fall into the latter category when your time comes.

Here is a way to begin that has been proven in my own life and with hundreds of
nurses in the real world of healthcare.

Time to do the "Big 180"

In order to see the way through, you must step out of your programming and make
a 180-degree shift in your awareness.

Move from avoiding the things you don't want …

… to figuring out what you really want …

… and going to get it.

> *No problem can be solved*
> *from the same level of consciousness that created it.*
> —*Albert Einstein*

I often get asked, "If I can just avoid all the things I don't want, I will get what I want … right?" What do you think the answer is?

Here is the reality

To get what you want, the steps you need to take will look something like this:

1. Take the time to decide what you want in your life and career.
2. Start taking baby steps in that direction, beginning to free up your purpose.
3. Wake up the dreams you tucked away when you entered nursing school.
4. Get off the tracks others have laid for you to follow.
5. Put nurse burnout to its highest and best use.

Burnout is here to nudge you onto a different path … one with more purpose. You really can decide what you want and go get it. You can set your own tracks from now on. You can use your discomfort to fuel your change.

The remainder of this book is devoted to giving you new levels of awareness and new tools. You will learn how to step off these rails of others' expectations. Let me show you how to recognize your own path and navigate its twists and turns toward your Ideal Nursing Career with intention and on purpose.

Perhaps you will become like that wise and respected mentor I asked you to think about at the beginning of this chapter. Perhaps you will share your burnout story with others down the road.

When you are ready to get started, let's take out the trash.

Burnout's highest and best use ACTION STEPS

- What do you really want at this point in your life and your career?
- Is now the time to take action and go get it?
- What new choices do you see available to you now?
- What are the benefits and consequences of each path you might take going forward?

CHAPTER 2

TAKE OUT THE HEAD TRASH

Five Changes in Awareness That Enable the Burnout Prevention Tools to Work

"It ain't what you don't know that gets you into trouble.
It's what you know for sure that just ain't so."
—Mark Twain

"We don't see things as they are, we see them as we are."
—Anaïs Nin

"He that will not apply new remedies must expect new evils."
—Francis Bacon

Head trash is the trash in your head. It is the crooked and inaccurate thought processes, the smoke and mirrors of your conditioning that get in your way without you knowing it. I have already shown you five flavors of programming and two prime directives that set every nurse up to be at extremely high risk for burnout. That is one category of head trash. Let me show you five additional, nurse-specific behavior patterns and world views that will also get in your way, so we can take them out to the Dumpster all at once.

<u>Do not skip this chapter.</u>

You must take out the trash before you have any chance of living on purpose. Empty the trash, and then we can instill the new tools that follow into the bright, shiny space you will create. Just like cleaning the kitchen before you prepare a new dish for the first time, taking out the head trash first provides you with a fresh start and a foundation for a new and upward spiral.

HEAD TRASH #1: DEAL WITH YOUR INNER CRITIC

AS YOU LEARN about burnout and contemplate new actions, you will probably notice a voice in your head now and then we can call your "inner critic." It is a part of your personality that judges you and can get in the way of taking new action steps. Its dominant emotion is usually guilt or shame.

Here are some examples of what your inner critic might whisper in your ear:

Jeez, why didn't you know this sooner? You are such an idiot.
You can't take time for yourself; that's selfish.
Like that is ever going to happen.
This is too difficult/simple/stupid/woo woo.
I am too busy for any of this.

Whatever your inner critic says, the key is to not let that little voice stop you from making the changes you are seeking. Try this first: When you hear the little voice trying to take you out, say to yourself, *Thank you for sharing*, and keep moving forward.

One of two things will happen:

1.) The inner critic will let you pass. It will come up again at some point, and your *thank you for sharing* **will be enough that it will step aside and allow you to proceed.**

If you find your inner critic is either absent or it does not stop you from moving forward, things are simpler. Carry on, full speed ahead. You can move on to the next section, Head Trash #2.

If Option 2 below is happening to you, please take a moment to read the next few paragraphs carefully.

2.) The inner critic will hijack you.

Let's look at this in some detail on the off chance this is happening to you right now.

What do I mean by "hijack?"

You will be stopped by a powerful negative emotion and not allowed to proceed. In your body, it feels the way a little kitten must feel when you grab it by the skin at the back of its neck and lift it off the floor.

- If you try *thank you for sharing* several times with your inner critic's objections, and it will not stand aside and let you proceed;

Or,

- If you are hijacked as above when trying to make changes, especially if this sense of panic seems familiar or you are unable to control your emotions;

You have legitimate reasons for a visit to a therapist or coach with experience in what is known as "parts work." This powerful inner critic is a "part" of your personality. "Parts work" is the name for a number of techniques that help you bring all the parts of your personality onto the same page and get them all pulling in the same direction.

In many of us, there is an inner critic that will not allow things to proceed until we upgrade our relationships with the critic. In most cases, something traumatic happened during nursing school or our professional years that resonates with trauma from childhood. It's important to recognize this kind of head trash right away. It is often difficult to take it out without some professional help.

If you try to Lone Ranger here, it is not uncommon to get stopped in your tracks or confused enough to give up on your attempts to change things for the better. I encourage you to ask for help and allow yourself to be supported in this situation, especially if you happen to be a man.

Please realize that in these situations, your inner critic is trying to protect you. It is a blunt and effective instrument to stop you in your tracks. It uses old tactics and phrases that probably sound familiar. It is afraid of changing because it doesn't understand that the changes you are trying to make will be good for both of you.

You and your coach or therapist can work on bringing your relationship with this inner critic up to adult standards. When this is done well, this same voice will transform into your biggest ally and a key inner source of advice and wisdom.

As a coach, I have done this work in my own life. Learning to work with my own inner critic and other parts of my personality was one of the keys to my recovery from burnout.

HEAD TRASH #2: REALIZE BURNOUT IS NOT A PROBLEM

BURNOUT IS A challenge to be sure. It is not a problem, though. Here's what I mean.

PROBLEMS HAVE SOLUTIONS.

When you apply the solution to a problem, what happens? The problem disappears, right?

Problem + solution = no problem

Example:

Here is the purest example of a problem I can think of for a professional nurse: an empty IV bag.

What happens as our patient's IV bag reaches near empty? You got it … we hang a new bag. In the world of a nurse, an IV bag is something we check on frequently.

There is no finer example of a one-step solution than the hanging of a new bag to a close-to-empty IV medication.

So, an empty IV bag is a problem you can solve.

You wash your hands, restart your patient's pump, smile, and thank the nursing gods that you got a simple problem like this in your workday.

What about burnout? Is there the equivalent of an IV pump you can use to restart burnout and make it go away? The answer is an obvious "no." There is no one-step, permanent solution here.

The important distinction

- The reason you can't find a one-step solution for burnout is *not* because burnout is impossible to prevent.
- The reason there is no solution is this—burnout is not a problem.
- Burnout is a *dilemma.*

di·lem·ma; *noun - A situation in which a difficult choice has to be made between* *two alternatives—especially when both alternatives are either undesirable or mutually incompatible.*

In common language, we speak of being on the "horns of a dilemma." A dilemma is a never-ending balancing act. Here's the burnout dilemma.

DILEMMA: PRODUCTIVITY VS. BURNOUT

If you push your productivity too hard, you burn out and productivity falls. What you and your employer are seeking is a healthy balance of solid productivity at work without driving your energy account balances below zero and causing burnout. This is true whether you are employed by a large organization or are self-employed.

How do you "solve" a dilemma?

The short answer here is you don't.

- You *solve* problems.
- You *manage* dilemmas.

Your ability to distinguish between problems and dilemmas is a key new skill that will allow you to treat and prevent burnout. This *problem vs. dilemma* distinction is one you must learn to see clearly in order to build a fulfilling, balanced life.

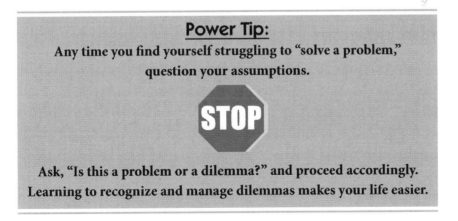

Power Tip:
Any time you find yourself struggling to "solve a problem,"
question your assumptions.

STOP

Ask, "Is this a problem or a dilemma?" and proceed accordingly.
Learning to recognize and manage dilemmas makes your life easier.

Four steps to managing a dilemma

Once you recognize you are facing a dilemma and not a problem—as in the case at hand, dealing with burnout—use these four steps to manage it effectively.

1. **DEFINE** the two horns and the optimum balance point.
2. Design a **STRATEGY** to create the balance you seek.

3. Build a **SYSTEM** to monitor the effectiveness of your strategy.

4. **TWEAK** your strategy and your system as often as needed.

THREE PROBLEM-SOLVING TRAPS FOR NURSES

We are problem solvers by our nature, our training, and our conditioning. We are always looking to find a solution to our patients' problems. We have a finely-honed sense of urgency as well. Because of the very nature of the pace of healthcare, we do everything we can to assess our patients and act on our evaluation in fifteen minutes or less.

We tend to see everything as a problem, and we derive our sense of worth and confidence from our ability to solve the problems around us.

Then, there's burnout. We make the mistake of thinking burnout is a problem too. We try to solve it over and over again and are unsuccessful. This is where a whole new layer of head trash tumbles in.

Rather than recognize burnout as a dilemma and work on a strategy, a large percentage of nurses will do one of these three things instead.

1.) Give Up

If you can't find a solution, it must be impossible to solve, right? You look all around and see many of your colleagues struggling in a similar fashion. Your programming has you work harder and try to figure this out all by yourself, despite your exhaustion. Eventually, many nurses simply give up on the possibility of having the life they want. Burnout is often a chronic condition.

2.) Play the Victim

Much more commonly, nurses slide into playing the role of the victim. I am not saying you are being victimized here. There is no perpetrator. No one is sitting in a smoke-filled room plotting to knock your life out of balance and deliberately torture you with EMR, staffing shortages, committee work, or patient satisfaction surveys.

Victim mode is a creeping change in your locus of control. You begin to believe you are not in charge of your life. You feel like you are swinging in the breeze, a helpless victim of the next administration order that comes down the pike.

The following behaviors are three signs you are playing the victim:

1. Blame
2. Justify
3. Complain

Any time you find yourself doing one of these things, you are playing the victim. In most cases, you missed a chance along the way to take more charge of your circumstances. Now, you feel stuck. You don't see a solution, so these three options feel like the only reasonable thing to do. This behavior is very common among nurses, as you well know.

Playing the victim is learned helplessness.

Blaming, justifying, and complaining never work. These three behaviors will never get you what you want. You will only alienate the very same people who could help you out of the downward spiral.

Did you know there is a popular conception in healthcare management circles that nurses are just a bunch of whiners? Listen to their stories and you will see that many administrators are bombarded with nurses who do nothing but walk into their office to blame, justify, and complain about everything. They want something to be done about the issue at hand, yet are unable to offer any suggestions. Or, what's worse—they don't even go to management but instead just gossip and complain in the break room to their colleagues about everything that's wrong with the workplace. The constant repetition of victim behaviors is what causes administrators to give up on burnout prevention and deal with nurse turnover instead.

Playing the victim is one of the few things that is more common in nurses than the symptoms of burnout themselves. This head trash has got to go if you are going to get more of what you want going forward.

You can un-learn this behavior.

Doing so will make a big difference for a simple reason. When you blame, justify, and complain, you are giving away your power to change things. Instead of figuring out what you want and making it happen, you are venting your discomfort and then going right back to the miserable status quo.

Playing the victim means you missed an opportunity to take charge. When you catch yourself in victim mode, you will realize that at some earlier point you had an opportunity to take more control of the situation and you missed it.

You might have noticed the opportunity come up, but you did not take it. Or, you might have missed it completely. Either way, recognizing you are playing the victim gives you a second chance to take charge. Ask yourself these questions:

- What do you really want to have happen here—instead of the thing you are complaining about?
- What would you have to do to get that different result?
- What is the smallest first step you can take to begin turning this around?
- When are you going to do *that* instead of blame, justify, and complain?

I encourage you to recognize the victim when it pops up. Use it as a sign to get crystal clear on what you want in this situation. Then, take charge of the situation as much as possible.

3.) Find a Work-Around

Everyone knows that nurses are notorious for finding work-arounds. It comes out of nurses' mouths when they say things like, "Oh, I know how we can get to those supplies without entering the code to the stock room."

There is no work-around here, especially when we talk about burnout. Here is my experience:

- The origin of burnout is always multifactorial.
- A successful strategy for the treatment and prevention of burnout is always multifactorial.
- Creating your ideal career and an amazing life is always multifactorial.

There is no one thing. There is no work-around and no shortcut, no matter how much you may wish for it. The work-around is a universal form of magical thinking. The key is to recognize the presence of a dilemma and focus on building an effective strategy to end the downward spiral. The good news is that your strategy will ultimately only have three to five components. All it takes is a small number of little changes to get you back on track to your ideal career.

<u>Let all the head trash go</u>

Treating or preventing burnout or building your ideal nursing career is always a combination of a number of little changes. Clean out your head trash and put together several new actions that get the results you are seeking.

As long as you remain focused on what you want and dedicated to taking action to implement the tools in your life, you will find that every new action produces a new result. The results of your new actions often add up in an exponential fashion. When you begin to live more on purpose and take actions to create your ideal practice, as little as two small changes can make a huge impact.

Get ready to put a number of things in play, one at a time. Then, you can sit back and watch the math of your new results take place.

Know you have a strategic partner now

Now that you understand burnout is a dilemma, you can recognize this book and the additional resources at *www.StopNurseBurnout.com/powertools* as potential building blocks for your strategy. Build your own personal strategy by picking and choosing the ones that work for you and trying them out in your own career and life. You will quickly learn which combination works best to reach your goals.

Burnout is not the only dilemma you are facing right now

I will point out additional dilemmas as we bump into them going forward. You will recognize them as stubborn places where you are struggling at the moment. Just to get you started, realize that electronic documentation and work-life balance are both dilemmas too. Go figure.

I will be reminding you to stop trying to solve dilemmas and work on effective strategies instead, giving you examples as we go along.

Taking out this head trash by calling out dilemmas when you see them is perhaps the most important trip to the dumpster of them all.

HEAD TRASH #3: DO THE BIG 180

WE TOUCHED ON this in the last chapter, and it is a piece of head trash that cannot be emphasized enough. In order to get what you want, you have to stop the natural and constant focus on avoiding what you don't want. You must practice cranking your attention around a full 180 degrees to focus on what you want instead.

We are hardwired at the level of the reticular activating system to be on the lookout for danger and threats. We have a default setting in our neuroanatomy to focus our awareness on our problems. We see the things that are not going right like giant neon lights on a dark night.

The conditioning of our nursing education then piles on to form a dense second layer of problem-focused awareness.

Example:

Imagine for a moment that you and I are standing side by side, leaning on the railing of the balcony at Grand Central Station in New York City, looking out over the thousands of people below bustling between trains. In the very same instant, we would both notice the single individual in the crowd who is limping. We would then proceed to get into a heated back-and-forth discussion over whether or not we should go help him onto the train.

You know this is true. I want you to know something clearly. Only nurses do that kind of thing. We might miss any number of sweet, tender, and touching things going on at the same time on the platform below—a father laughing with his toddler, the sound of a violin wafting out of one of the tunnels.

To us, the slight limp seventy-five yards away in the crowd is a flashing red light in our awareness. Our attention turns to this sign of abnormal physiology like a moth is attracted to a flame. This ability to spot a situation to care for others is a valuable skill, but only in certain settings. Constant focus on problems and our ability to serve others gives you a specific experience of life. I encourage you to experiment with the big 180 and practice noticing what is going right instead.

Focus on what you want

Building your ideal practice and a balanced life does not come from solving problems. The key is to focus on what you want.

- When you focus on your problems, your attention is occupied by the things you don't want.
- When you focus on your problems, you are looking for things to run away from and avoid.
- Focusing only on the negativity in your life is going to attract more negativity.
- You can fix all your problems and still not get what you want in your life.
- You can toss out this head trash and learn to take a 180-degree turn in your energy and awareness by focusing instead on what you really want - and heading in *that* direction.

Rise above neuroanatomy and programming

I encourage you to rise above the basic reflexes of your reticular activating system and your nursing programming and set aside some regular time to focus on what you want.

- I know you took a lot of your dreams and desires and did the spiritual equivalent of stuffing them deep in your back pocket when you entered nursing school. We all did. You knew you were entering into an educational track that would take years, so you put your dreams away for a later date. Check your back pocket. They are still there.
- And I understand no one else has ever asked you what you really want, and you probably don't think about it much, given how busy you are.
- Now is a time when you can choose to wake those dreams and desires back up again. You can use them to generate clarity and power as you learn to deal with the dilemmas around you.

The singer Joe Jackson lays out the reality as simply as possible:

> *You can't get what you want till you know what you want.*
> —Joe Jackson

Once you know what you really want, you can build an action plan to go straight at it. Your desire for this goal will pull you forward. You will be running toward something positive, instead of running away from something negative. Your attention will be occupied by things you desire, by the life you hope to create. With this as your focus and power source, I promise you will make progress.

HEAD TRASH #4: RELEASE THE SUPERHERO— SPIN PLATES INSTEAD

YOU ARE A nurse. You are a person who sees problems and helps fix them. Your super-hero sense of urgency is very overdeveloped. After all, under normal circumstances, you only have fifteen minutes or so to assess patients and give them their medications before getting pulled to another room or the next part of your assignment.

The biggest temptation when you are reading this book will be to try to do too much at once. This is a recipe for overwhelm for one simple reason. You are probably close enough to overwhelm right now that it wouldn't take much to drive you right over the edge. I would hate this book to be the last straw.

Spin plates instead

Remember the *Ed Sullivan Show*? He is rightly famous for introducing the Beatles, Rolling Stones, and others to US television audiences. But, he also had a number of acts that seem ludicrously primitive by today's standards. One of them was a man named Erich Brenn. Mr. Brenn made a living as a plate spinner. You can search his name on YouTube and find the video of the full performance.

He took plates and bowls and spun them atop long dowels until he had thirteen of them going at once.

One plate at a time

The secret to the act was simple. He spun up one plate at a time and didn't move on to the second one until plate number one was going full speed.

When you get to the tools section of this book, make sure you follow his plate spinning lead. Think about your strategy, and know you will be using 3-5 tools by the time your strategy is fully formed. Then pick a tool—just one—and get it spinning full speed and fully operational in your career and life before moving on to number two.

Do not overload yourself by taking on multiple action steps at once. It is a recipe for failure and a mind trap of our perfectionist, workaholic, superhero programming.

HEAD TRASH #5: CELEBRATE ALL WINS

YOUR NURSE-FOCUS ON problems will often cause low-level worry and suffering in your life. You may get a lot done in your day, but instead of celebrating what you have accomplished, you focus instead on the next undone task on your list. We constantly judge ourselves and find something missing. This version of our perfectionist program goes much deeper, though, and it doesn't stop with us.

Not only do we focus on what is not working, we constantly judge ourselves and all the people around us for missing the mark. Nurses often mistake this flavor of head trash for doing a good job and keeping everyone on their toes. It is neither. If all you are doing is seeing what is going wrong and judging people for it, this habitual thought process will drive people away from you and steer your quality of life right into the ditch. There is another way.

You can cultivate the ability to see what is working—see Head Trash #3 above. Then go one step further.

Learn to acknowledge and celebrate and be happy for the things that are going right. A huge body of research from the organizational development and parenting literature shows that this mindset is key to new levels of effectiveness as a leader.[6] It is nothing more than your nurse programming keeping you laser-focused on what is going wrong, just like watching the limping man in Grand Central Station.

In reality, whenever you see a problem or something going wrong, 95 percent of the time there is something right happening in the same moment. You can develop the skill of acknowledging what you and all the people around you have accomplished, rather than focusing only on what remains undone.

When you take on these habit patterns, you put a completely different driver at the wheel of your quality of life.

You don't have to give up being a good nurse to be a happier person.

It is important to note that you don't have to deny your ability to identify and solve problems to accomplish this task. You can be a great patient advocate and the first to point out the patient's needs and, at the same time, acknowledge what you or your staff member is doing well.

Here is why it is so important to take out this piece of head trash: if all you do is focus on what is wrong, you are being too hard on yourself, and you are a pain in the rear to everyone on your team. You are difficult to please and a real task master. The tragedy is you probably don't realize it. It slows you and everyone around you down. It is the essence of the phrase, "nose to the grindstone."

You grind your face off with a relentless focus on fixing problems and putting out fires, and it just does not have to be that way. In fact, there is plenty of research evidence that acknowledging what is going right on your team is a key to peak performance.[7]

Let me show you three ways to take out this head trash. Each one is an awareness-shifting tool you can use on yourself and the people around you to keep your energy up and make the journey to your goals a pleasant one from now on.

1.) Treat Yourself Like a Dog

Do you have a dog? Have you ever had one? Think of that dog now. If you don't have a dog, think of the cutest dog you can. For me, it is always a lab puppy or my pit bull, Rusty.

If you came home and that dog met you at the door, eyes bright and tail wagging, what would you do?

You'd probably say something along the lines of, "Aren't you a good boy?" and give him a scratch behind the ears. You'd be pleased he met you at the door and greeted you in such a fashion. You would show your pleasure in clear and obvious ways—ways we often reserve exclusively for our pets.

Now, think of the last time you had a task list at work and you completed one of the tasks. How did you treat yourself? What did you do before you moved on to the next item on the list?

Most nurses will answer, "Nothing—I just moved on to the next thing." Some of us cross the item off with a pen or check a box, but there is no further acknowledgment, no scratch behind the ear.

Take a look at these two situations and you will immediately notice:

- You treat your dog better than you do yourself.
- If you treated your dog the way you treat yourself, your dog would probably go live with your neighbor.

"Treat Yourself Like a Dog" means "Celebrate All Wins"

Why don't you acknowledge yourself when you complete an item on your task list? Why not do a little fist pump or a couple steps of your happy dance? It is just a habit. There are two main categories of habits, and I don't mean the good and the bad.

1. Habits of doing
2. Habits of not doing

You simply have a habit of *not* celebrating your accomplishments. It is a habit of not doing. That is an exhausting habit, especially since there are dozens of things you could be celebrating every single day, like doing a good job with a patient, completing a chart, helping a member of your team, reading to your children, or the experience of your dog coming to meet you at the door. There are so many positive things to celebrate and acknowledge in your day. You won't see them, though, until you rise above your programming to actually be on the lookout for them.

Just like you and I could look out over Grand Central Station and see the man buying his wife flowers instead of the one who is limping.

I encourage you to develop the habit of noticing and celebrating all wins. Do it for yourself. Do it for your team. Do it for your family.

2.) The Gap vs. Progress

In any situation where you are trying to reach a goal, the following graphic applies.

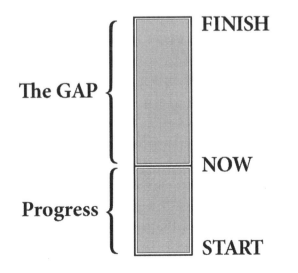

You have a starting point, and the goal is your finish line. At some point, you will be part way there. This sets up two spaces in the diagram.

1. There is a space between where you started and where you are. Let's call that "progress."
2. There is a space between where you are and the finish line. Let's call that "the gap."

Which one of these spaces do you notice first?

You are programmed to see the gap more clearly than progress. This is because the gap is the problem. The gap is what is going wrong. We focus on the gap so strongly; it is common to completely ignore or give only passing lip service to progress. We do this with ourselves, our staff, our patients, and our family. The only place we don't have this habit pattern is with our pets—hence, "treat yourself like a dog."

Develop the habit of noticing and celebrating progress first.

You will reach your goals more easily and have more fun along the way. Develop this same habit with your patients, staff, and family, and you will become a better nurse, leader, spouse or significant other, and parent.

I am not saying you should be all *happy, happy, joy, joy* and ignore the gap. Let's both be realistic here. The gap is the work that has to be done to reach our ultimate goal. Don't ignore or minimize it. Keep the patient and the team organized around closing the gap and reaching your goal. What I am saying is:

- Notice and celebrate progress *first.*
- Congratulate anyone on any progress *first.*
- Reward yourself and others on your accomplishments *first.*

Then, turn to the gap and the issue of how to close it.

Work on the gap; don't beat yourself and everyone up with it.

A patient care example:

Imagine you receive your patient assignment for the day. You notice you have Mr. Jones in room 24. Wait, what's that? Mr. Jones was just discharged five days ago. And he's back again? How can this be? You remember carefully teaching him about the two new medications that were started during his last hospital stay. He had new onset congestive heart failure and had never needed to take regular medication before that discharge. Things were going so well when he left. You note his orders and medications for the morning, put on a smiling face, and enter his room.

> *You: "How are you today, Mr. Jones? Back to see us again … what happened?"*
> *Mr. Jones: "I am alright. Didn't sleep so well last night. I know this is my fault. I remembered my morning pills just fine, but I just couldn't remember to take those new pills at night. Things just got worse, and I couldn't breathe."*

What would you say next?

Our nurse programming will have us see what is going wrong like a red light flashing in the room. You can see the gap, right? You can see what is not going right. You may be getting ready to jump all over the fact that he missed his evening medication with both feet first. I call that *beating him up with the gap* because that is what it feels like to the patient.

My strongest suggestion is you look for something going right in this situation and find a way to treat him like a dog. If you treat him like a dog first - celebrate progress - and look for ways to build on what is working, two things will happen. Mr. Jones will engage with you and his treatment plan more effectively, and you will have a much more positive and less stressful experience of this patient encounter.

If you listen closely to what Mr. Jones said, he was able to remember the morning dose of his new medication. He wasn't on any medicines when he came into the hospital last time. He left on two. He is a man who has never taken a regular medication before and he somehow remembered to take one of the two. Here's something going right we can work with.

It could go something like this:

> *You: "Well, Mr. Jones, great job remembering that morning dose of your medicine. I know it was not an easy thing because that was a new pill for you—great work.*
> *• Now, exactly how did you remember to take it in the morning?*
> *• What did you learn on that morning dose that can help you remember the evening one?*
> *• Is there anyone or anything else that can help you remember the evening dose?"*

Let him answer those questions one at a time. Acknowledge his problem solving here. Treat him like a dog, and give him a high five for these new ideas.

When you seek out what is working first—find the things that are going right in the situation—and jump all over them instead, you will find things get easier and more enjoyable very quickly. Always work to rise above your nurse programming and treat your patients like dogs.

3.) The Satisfaction Mind Flip

- Think about your career and the way things have been going over the last month or so.
- Rate your level of satisfaction with your career on a scale of 0–10 (*0 = it couldn't get any worse* and *10 = it couldn't get any better*).
- What is your level of satisfaction?
- Is it going up or down?
- How does that number feel?

Notice how your awareness is focused on the problems that keep this score from being a ten. This is a perfect example of how you see the gap first.

When you see your score, what you almost certainly see first is the gap between your score and a ten. If I ask you to list the reasons your satisfaction is not a ten, they come rolling off your tongue in a free-flowing and detailed problem list.

Let's flip your mind here

Here is the question that triggers the Satisfaction Mind Flip:

Why is your satisfaction score NOT A ZERO?

Grab a sheet of paper and write down *all the reasons you didn't give your career a zero satisfaction score.*

You know what this list is, yes? It is all the things that are going right in the workplace. These are the things you can build on to give you higher levels of satisfaction more quickly than you can imagine.

The quickest way to lower your stress and find more fulfillment in your practice and balance in your life is to figure out what is going right and do more of that.

The full triad

1. Treat Yourself Like a Dog—Celebrate All Wins
2. Focus on Progress First—Don't just beat yourself and others up with the Gap
3. Notice What is Going Right—The Satisfaction Mind Flip

NOTE:

There are reams of scientific evidence for the effectiveness of these three tools in building high-performing teams and in being a more effective parent and a happier, more fulfilled, and joyful person. In organizational development, this is called "Appreciative Inquiry." In parenting, it is called "catch your kids doing something right." I encourage you to take out this head trash and instill a new habit of noticing and celebrating all wins. You and everyone around you will appreciate it.

TAKE OUT THE HEAD TRASH SUMMARY

1. Recognize and deal with your inner critic. Get help if you need it.
2. Realize burnout is not a problem—it is a dilemma. Focus on building a strategy for balance.
3. Do the BIG 180—focus on what you want, not what you don't want.
4. Release the superhero—spin plates instead.
5. Celebrate all wins.

Take out the head trash ACTION STEPS

- What are the common things your inner critic says to slow you down?
- How does the distinction between a problem and a dilemma show up in other areas of your life?
- Make a list of the things that are going right in your life at this present moment.
- Where could you make more progress by spinning a plate and focusing on doing a good job with just one thing in your practice or life?
- What progress have you made toward a recent goal? How did you do that?
- How would you like to celebrate it? (A fist pump right now is probably a good start.)
- When will you do that?
- Journal on these questions.

CHAPTER 3

YOUR IDEAL CAREER

Building Your Blueprint and Master Plan For Change

"We are called to be architects of the future, not its victims."
—Buckminster Fuller

*"When I'm working on a problem, I never think about beauty.
I only think about how to solve the problem. But, when I have finished,
if the solution is not beautiful, I know it is wrong."*
—Buckminster Fuller

AIM HIGHER

When you recognize your own dissatisfaction or burnout and use it to make changes in your career, you can aim high or you can aim low. Most people aim low. When you are in survival mode, all you can focus on is something to ease your stress levels and treat or prevent symptomatic burnout. Better is good enough and just reversing burnout is probably all you are hoping for. That is aiming low.

I encourage you to aim higher.

The tools in the remainder of this book can be used to accomplish all of those basic goals. You can lower your stress and treat or prevent burnout with every tool from here on out. They work when applied to that purpose.

If you aim higher, they can also be used to reach the ultimate goal—building your Ideal Career and a rich and fulfilling life.

This is another example where you can rise above your nurse programming. You have the ability to do the BIG 180 shift in your awareness here too. You can move away from simple problem solving and focus on what you really want. That will seem a little foreign at first, I am sure. I encourage you to do it anyway.

It is not uncommon for me to ask overstressed nurses what they really want their career to look like in an ideal world and be met with a slack-jawed, blank stare. The

72

reply is generally along the lines of, "I don't know. No one has ever asked me that question."

That's because no one else has ever cared. As long as you are a train on someone else's tracks, all they care about is you doing their bidding. You are fulfilling their agenda. What you want has never been a consideration. Your desires are of no concern to your nursing school, professional orientation, or your employer.

At the same time, you have always had wiggle room in your career to shift things more toward what you really want. You just weren't aware of it until now.

Check your aim here and let's shoot for the bull's-eye of your Ideal Career rather than just some minor stress relief. Are you ready?

YOUR IDEAL CAREER DESCRIPTION

"You don't get what you want in life. You get what you tolerate."
—Anurag Gupta

THE FIRST STEP in creating your Ideal Career is simple: build your Ideal Career Description (ICD). Your ICD is your ultimate goal, your vision, the bull's-eye in your target. It is something you can run toward and allow to pull you forward, rather than continuously running away from the things you don't want.

KEYS TO CREATING A POWERFUL IDEAL CAREER DESCRIPTION

Write it down.

I am old-school here, and I admit it. I encourage you to get a manila folder and label it "My Ideal Career Description."

Use your favorite pen to write down the description of your Ideal Career—your dream job—and keep this description in the manila folder. I love taking out that folder on a quiet Sunday morning and updating it. If you are more comfortable with a tablet computer and an electronic document, go that direction. The important thing here is that you have a fully fleshed-out Ideal Career Description to organize your next steps.

Your Ideal Career Description answers these questions:

If you had a magic wand and could wave it to pop your Ideal Career into existence right here in front of you …

- What kinds of patients do you want to see?
  - What different kinds of people?
  - What age group?
  - What specialty?
- In what setting?
  - Hospital, academia, outpatient care, long-term treatment, or in the community?

➤ Do you want to work in a school, at a physician's office, with legal documentation, or in nursing informatics?
- For how many hours in the week and on what schedule?
- For what pay?
  ➤ What is the minimum pay you must receive each month to support your family and your lifestyle?
- In what kind of a group?
  ➤ Would you like to work with a team, remotely from home, or on your own?
- Of what size?
- With what kind of a group culture?
- How would you describe your ideal boss and his or her communication and leadership style?
- How does this group make decisions?
- Where do you want your career to be located?
  ➤ In an urban or rural setting?
  ➤ In what area of the country or the world?
  ➤ With what recreational activities available to you?

It is your magic wand. Wave it. Imagine your Ideal Career. Write it all down. Don't leave something off the list if a little voice is telling you it is impossible. Say, *thank you for sharing*, and write it down anyway. Your Ideal Career is something to aspire to, so put it all down here.

<u>DO NOT SKIP THIS STEP.</u>

- Your Ideal Career Description is unique to you.
- It is your personal blueprint for building a more Ideal Career.
- Once you are clear on your Ideal Career Description, the next two steps will allow you to quickly build an action plan to get there.

Your clarity here organizes all the steps that follow. Be patient and give yourself time to get clear on your own personal Ideal Career Description now.

Working as a nurse without an ideal job description is like building a house without a blueprint.

Imagine, for a second, trying to build a house without a blueprint. Just imagine you go to town, buy a truck full of wood, come home, and start putting up walls with no blueprint. What kind of a house would you end up with… no matter how hard you worked at it?

You may have been doing exactly that up until now with your career. You have made choices over time without a plan and here, ten years later, is the result. This process will allow you to pick your head up and realize—when you compare your current situation to your ideal—this career didn't make sense then and makes even less sense now.

<u>DO NOT SKIP THIS STEP (it is worth repeating). Without your ideal career description, you have no blueprint, no target, no bull's eye.</u>

You don't know where you are headed, *and* you cannot complete the next step: creating the *Master Plan* for this building project.

THREE THINGS TO KNOW ABOUT YOUR IDEAL CAREER DESCRIPTION

1.) Getting Clear on Your Ideal Career is a Process.

This is a process. It takes time.

It normally takes a period of days to weeks to get clear on what you really want in your Ideal Career. No one has ever asked you these questions before. It takes a while to recognize your programming and allow your dreams to wake up. Here's what I mean.

At some point back in your education, you had a dream of what it would be like to be a professional nurse. Take a second right now to think back on that dream. Now, look around at your current reality. You probably notice that old dream and your current reality don't overlap as well as you would like.

That dream has been asleep for a while. You were never taught how to use it as a meaningful target. You were never taught the steps to actually bring it to life. There may even be a piece of you that has given up on the dream entirely.

It takes a while to wake your dream up, wipe off the guilt that sometimes tarnishes its surface these years later, and write it down.

Be patient with yourself. Keep picking up the folder, taking out your ICD, and adding and subtracting as things pop into your mind.

Along the way, there may be a little voice in your head saying things like, *What makes you think you are so special?* Or, *Nobody gets everything they want; you should be satisfied with what you have.*

Do you recognize that as your inner critic?

You can tell these voices, *Thank you for sharing,* and keep building your Ideal Career Description. It is your programming speaking. Now, it is your turn to decide consciously what your Ideal Career and life is and start living with purpose.

You deserve this

Understand very clearly:

- You deserve this.
- You have earned it.
- Now is your time.

Creating your Ideal Career Description is the first step in the process of living the dreams you held so hopefully way back at the beginning.

If you are just starting out

If you are currently a nursing student, in orientation, or in your first few years of your career, the Ideal Career Description is even more important. Write down that dream *now* so you can maintain your focus and bring it to life ASAP.

2.) **Your Ideal Career is a Moving Target.**

Your Ideal Career Description is not a static list of requirements. It is always changing, sometimes gradually and sometimes with stunning speed.

- Your ICD when you are single is different than when you have children.
- Your ICD is different when you are fifty-five than when you are thirty-five.
- Your ICD is different again when your kids are all grown and moved out.

What you feel to be your Ideal Career may change dramatically overnight if a parent becomes ill and must move in with you, or any one of hundreds of similar life-altering events take place.

No matter what your age and situation, clarity on your ICD is a critical piece of your burnout prevention strategy and a key to actually building your Ideal Career. You must review and tweak it regularly.

How often should you update your ICD?

From now on, make sure you update your ICD at least quarterly at a bare minimum—monthly is even better. Take the papers out, use a different color pen, and add and subtract as necessary.

3.) Your Ideal Career is an Ideal.

Your ICD is something to aspire to. Realize almost no one will have a job that perfectly matches his or her ideal. So, if there is something you want to put on your Ideal Career Description that is either difficult or impossible to achieve, put it in there anyway. Don't let the sarcastic voice of *Like that will ever happen!* stop you.

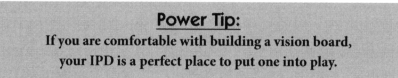

Power Tip:
If you are comfortable with building a vision board, your IPD is a perfect place to put one into play.

Example: my ideal life story

You can expand this process to create your Ideal Life as well. It all starts with doing the BIG 180 and getting clear on what you really want.

When I was newly graduated from my dual master's degrees, looking for a new job that would use my talents and skills, I used this very same process without knowing it. I talked with my academic advisor almost weekly and told her how I wanted a job in wellness and prevention, teaching people about health, even though it seemed impossible.

My list: I wanted to shift my work focus from tertiary care to primary prevention. I was looking to teach people about total well-being and ways they could remain healthy. I wanted a job with flexibility, responsibility, and independence.

I ended up leaving my full-time role as a psychiatric nurse to run a monitored exercise program at a wellness center. I was able to teach people about healthy habits and lifestyles with a great level of autonomy. Everything I imagined worked out, even though at the time I didn't put any formal visioning process into place. In hindsight, I was able to write down the steps of this powerful process so I could share them here with you.

If there is *anything* you want in your career or your life, I encourage you to put it on your Ideal Career Description. Do the BIG 180, get clear on what you really want, and let's go get it. Your clarity is power.

THE NURSE'S VENN OF HAPPINESS

ONCE YOU HAVE your Ideal Career Description in hand, you can build the following Venn diagram to help you bring it to life. I call this the "Nurse's Venn of Happiness" because it will show you the shortest path from where you are now to a more Ideal Career.

This simple diagram will give you power and precision you have not possessed until now.

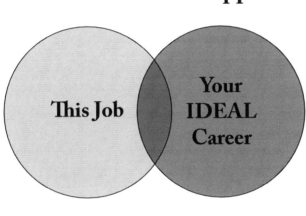

Nurse's VENN of Happiness

Maximize the Overlap

What is your current overlap?

When you are clear on your Ideal Career Description, take a look at the Venn of Happiness above. Notice how much overlap it feels you have between your current role and your ICD. This is a feeling more than a calculation. Write it down as a percentage.

Example:

It feels like there is about a 35 percent overlap between this role and my Ideal Career.

When I am working with nurses who are well into the downward spiral of burnout, they will tell me the overlap is in the 15-25 percent range.

Most nurses are very satisfied with their current job when the overlap is in the 60 percent and above range. When your overlap is 60 percent, you have a fundamental alignment with your ICD and the rest is just fine-tuning.

Your professional goal is to maximize the overlap.

The Venn of Happiness gives you the power to move in the direction of your Ideal Career more quickly than you might imagine possible.

All you have to do is answer a supremely simple question to create the Master Plan for building your Ideal Career.

THE MASTER PLAN QUESTION

WHAT WOULD YOU change about this job to increase the overlap with your Ideal Career?

Normally, when I ask this question to a client, they are able to make a detailed list quickly and easily. You know the stress points and the things that just don't work the way they should at work. From now on don't just keep this list in your head.

Write these changes down.

Make a list of your answers to that question. Write down as many changes as you can think of—even if you think they are impossible. *Get all these ideas out of your head and down on paper.*

This list is your Master Plan for building your Ideal Career.

This is the master list of improvement projects for your career going forward. Keep them in the folder with your written Ideal Career Description. This is a very specific list that grants you what can feel somewhat like a super power. Here's what I mean. Each time you make progress on even one of the changes on your Master Plan, you increase the overlap in the Venn of Happiness, automatically lower your stress levels, and build a more Ideal Career.

This is also the escape hatch from Einstein's Insanity Trap. The changes on your Master Plan will require new actions. Simply put, if you want different results you must take different actions. Your Master Plan shows you new ways forward to your ICD.

Every single nurse's Master Plan is as unique as your fingerprints.

This list and your Ideal Career Description are a customized, highly specific plan you can follow to treat and prevent burnout. If you aim high enough, they will also help you build your Ideal Career and a much more balanced life.

Use your Master Plan to select your tools.

A carpenter has to look at the blueprint to select the appropriate tools and materials he will take to the job site on any given day. The same principle applies for you in this Ideal Career construction project. Use your Master Plan to decide which of the tools in Chapter 4 are most appropriate for you.

Use your Master Plan to select your action steps.

With your Master Plan and appropriate tools in hand, you can focus like a laser on taking the most powerful actions. You can increase the overlap on your Venn of Happiness rapidly as you spin these plates of focused action one at a time.

Before you proceed further, take these two steps now:

1. Take at least a first pass on your Ideal Career Description.
2. Take at least a first pass on your Master Plan to increase the overlap in the Venn of Happiness.

If you need to, put this book down, grab a pen and your favorite beverage, and do that now.

TWO WARNINGS

1.) One Step at a Time

As nurses, we have a finely tuned sense of urgency. One large danger to your progress here is to bite off more than you can chew right at the start.

You may be very excited at this point. You have your Ideal Career Description and Master Plan in hand. You can probably visualize some clear steps to align that Venn diagram. Before you jump right in …

Remember plate spinning.

The temptation is to try to change a bunch of things at once. Don't do it. Remember, you are already busy to the point of overload. Recall the concept of plate spinning for a moment. One plate at a time … right?

Here is a way to take your list of changes and make progress without risking overload.

Look at your Master List of the changes you want to make.

- Prioritize them and *pick just one.*
  - ‣ You may be a person who picks the biggest change first or someone who picks the easiest to start with. I recommend going with the easiest, simplest, and quickest change first. You are making changes *and* building your change-making muscles here at the same time. I encourage you to tackle a simple project first. Harvest the low-hanging fruit and build your skills before you take on a bigger project that demands more of you and your team.

- Review the tools in Chapter 4 and see which one best fits your needs.
- Then, plan your action step.
- What is the simplest thing you can do—the smallest first step—to put that change in action?
- When are you going to get it done?
- Get out your calendar and schedule it.
- Do it.
- Celebrate - actually pump your fist and say "Yes!" or give yourself a pat on the back. Treat yourself like a dog and celebrate all wins from this point forward.
- Once the first change is complete and you have this plate spinning nice and fast, take a look at your list and get started on the next thing.
- Journal on your experience on several different levels:
  ‣ What was the change you made and what difference do you notice now?
  ‣ What was your experience of consciously changing your career to build a more satisfying work experience?
  ‣ What did you learn?
  ‣ What will you do differently as you make your next career change?

2.) Beware of Magical Thinking

Notice what comes up in your head the first time you look at the Venn of Happiness and ask the Master Plan question: *What would I change about this job to increase the overlap with my Ideal Career?*

If a little voice in your head says something sarcastic like, *Get rid of EMR,* I encourage you to notice that is magical thinking. EMR is not going away. We both know that is true, right?

It is okay and normal to have those thoughts; however, your Master Plan is better served by taking out that head trash and substituting a statement you can work with.

Something like:

- Spend less time on documentation.
- Always have my charting done when I leave my shift—and leave within thirty minutes of giving report.

As you work on this Master Plan item, you can see there are any number of ways to reach that goal, whereas "get rid of EMR" is magical thinking that just keeps you stuck in resentment and burnout.

BUILDING YOUR IDEAL CAREER SUMMARY

1. Create your Ideal Career Description
2. Build the Nurses Venn of Happiness
3. Ask the following question to create your Master Plan: "What would you change about this job to increase the overlap with your Ideal Career?"
4. Write down your list of answers. This is your Master Plan.

Building your Ideal Career ACTION STEPS

- Create a folder (real or electronic) to store these core documents.
  - ➤ Label it "My Ideal Career Description"
- Take a first pass at your Ideal Career Description.
  - ➤ Use colored pens, have some fun
  - ➤ Keep it in your folder
- Use the Venn of Happiness Diagram to estimate your current overlap in percent.
  - ➤ Write that percentage down. This is your starting point.
- Ask, "What would I change about this job to increase the overlap with my Ideal Career?"
- Label a document with "Master Plan" and write down all your answers.
  - ➤ Keep this in your folder too.
- Bring this folder, the ICD, and Master Plan to each of your weekly Strategy Sessions (see next chapter).
- Great work … Now, treat yourself like a dog.
  - ➤ You have laid the groundwork to create your ideal career on purpose.
  - ➤ Pump your fist and say "YES!" like you mean it.
  - ➤ Pat yourself on the back.
  - ➤ You now have your completely customized blueprint and Master Plan in hand.
- In the chapters ahead, use these documents to choose the tools for your Ideal Career building strategy.
- Commit to reviewing and updating these documents a minimum of quarterly—monthly, if possible.
- Journal on your experience.

CHAPTER 4

THE TOOLS

Field-Tested Tools to Prevent Burnout and Build Your Ideal Career

"If you only have a hammer,
you tend to see every problem as a nail."
—Abraham Maslow

"No sooner do we think we have assembled a comfortable life
than we find a piece of ourselves that has no place to fit in."
—Gail Sheehy

"Life begins at the end of your comfort zone."
—Neale Donald Walsch

<u>Here we go: the tools section. Let's review what we have covered so far.</u>

- You understand burnout's symptoms, causes, effects, pathophysiology, and complications.
- You know burnout's highest and best use.
- You have liberated yourself from several pounds of head trash.
- You understand burnout is a dilemma not a problem, and we are focused on building a multi-part strategy to address it.
- You have a journal where you are reflecting on the ways all this new learning shows up in your life.
- You have a folder labeled "My Ideal Career Description"—either hard copy or in an electronic format.
  - ❯ Inside is your first pass at a description of your Ideal Career.
- You understand the Nurse's Venn of Happiness.
- You have your Master Plan list written down and in that folder as well.
  - ❯ You have your initial list of changes that would align your career more with your Ideal Career.

Congratulations!

This is an enormous amount of progress given where you started. Take a breath or two now to congratulate yourself. I encourage you to reach your hand over one of your shoulders and give yourself a pat on the back. Treat yourself like a dog. You deserve it.

> **Power Tip:**
> Give up the superhero and Lone Ranger right away. Do not keep your exploration of your Ideal Career a secret. Use your team instead. This is important stuff that comes straight from your heart. Let others support you from the beginning.

- I encourage you to recruit a support team for your transition. Share this book, your ICD, and your Master Plan with your spouse or significant other and/or your colleagues at work. You can pool your efforts to make the changes all of you would like to see. Sooner or later, you will be asking all of them to help you. Why not do that now, at the beginning of this process? Their help in brainstorming and sharing the action plan could make a huge difference right away.
- Consider assembling a study group of colleagues to work the steps together. You can support each other and build brainstorming and accountability partnerships to accelerate movement toward your Ideal Career.

The four sections of this chapter hold a set of field-tested tools you can use to build your strategy for a more Ideal Career. Along the way, you will also lower your stress levels, increase your ability to recharge, and prevent burnout.

Remember, burnout is a *dilemma*. You are building a *strategy* here.

There is no quick fix or single step that works like magic. This toolbox is a place where you can use your own Ideal Career Description and Master Plan to pick and choose tools for your strategy, and know each and every tool has been tested and proven effective in the real world.

Remember to spin plates. When you are ready for action, make sure you only pick one tool at a time. Just one.

How do you choose which tools to use?

This process is a much like building a house. You have your Ideal Career Description in hand, and you have used the Venn of Happiness to create your Master Plan of changes you would like to make. You already hold the Blueprint and Project List for this new "house" you are going to build.

- **Your Ideal Career Description is the blueprint for this new home.** Everyone's blueprint is unique. It is your responsibility to keep your Ideal Career Description alive and up-to-date.

- **The Master Plan provides you with your Project List.** Here is the series of changes you must make to build the house in the blueprint. Just like a house plan has many components—wiring, plumbing, framing, flooring—your Project List will involve addressing the key elements that must change to build your Ideal Career. You will probably build strategies to address job stresses, work-life balance, EMR, and other issues. Everyone's Ideal Career Master List is unique. It is your responsibility to use the Venn of Happiness to create and prioritize your Master Plan.

- **The individual tools you are about to learn are the bricks and mortar, lumber and nails, for this building project.** These are the basic building blocks of new awareness and new actions needed to build your Ideal Career.

Before we get to the actual tools, let me give you a suggestion on how to start and nurture this project, as well as a framework for understanding the tools that follow.

COMMIT TO REGULAR STRATEGY SESSIONS

MOST NURSES I work with didn't burn out yesterday, recognize it immediately, and then call me for a consultation today. Burnout is not something you recognize right away. This is one of the classic "frog in a pot" situations where you don't notice the problem until it has been around for a long time.

We get too busy dealing with the sheer volume of activities required to practice as nurses and live our lives that we lose all perspective. We are too busy to pick our heads up and notice what is going on, much less change things around us.

You must work *ON* your career, not just *IN* it.

In order to make the changes you want, you must set aside time to step out of your routine and look down on your life and career from a strategic perspective. Only when you step out of the whirlwind of your day-to-day routine can you see the patterns that keep you stuck and begin to ask questions like:

- What do I really want?
- How are things going so far?
- What is working and what is not?
- What do I want to change?
- When will I take the first step?

How much time will you need?

I suggest you devote a minimum of one hour every other week to your own personal strategy session. This is the *minimum* amount to create momentum toward your Ideal Career you will be able to feel. If you want to move faster, schedule one hour *each* week.

Suggested strategy session agenda:

1. Get out your Ideal Career Description and Master Plan.
2. Have pen and paper or an open word-processing document at hand for notes and ideas.
3. Review and update your Ideal Career Description.
4. Review the Venn of Happiness and your Master Plan.
5. Review progress on your action steps from last week.

➤ Celebrate all wins and effort from last week.

6. Use your Master Plan to prioritize and study one tool in this book.

➤ The ACTION STEP list following each tool will guide your study and the translation of your new knowledge into meaningful actions.

7. Schedule your action steps for the week ahead.

➤ What Master Plan project are you addressing now? What action comes next?

➤ What ACTION STEP for which tool would you like to take in this coming week? You may be practicing the same tool week-to-week or picking up a new one. What is this week's step?

8. Schedule your next Strategy Session.

➤ This Strategy Session is not complete until your next one is on your calendar.

9. Journal in between Strategy Sessions. Some of your most important observations are fleeting. If you don't journal with some regularity here, you may not make progress as quickly as you would like.

➤ Keep track of your actions and the results of your new actions.

➤ Keep track of your feelings as you try new things. What patterns of head trash are the most common for you and what are you doing to release or get around it?

➤ Notice what works and what doesn't, what helps you be consistent, and what gets in your way.

➤ Review your journal notes as part of your Strategy Sessions.

THE BURNOUT PREVENTION MATRIX: ORIENTATION TO THE TOOLS

LET'S RECALL THE simple energetic rules that govern burnout.

- Burnout is caused by stress.
  - › Stress drains your energy accounts (physical, emotional, and spiritual).
  - › If you are unable to recharge your energy accounts, they will eventually fall to a negative balance.
  - › When your energy accounts fall into negative balance, burnout symptoms kick in.
  - › "You can't give what you ain't got."
- The five sources of stress and causes of burnout are:
  - › The profession: the stress of the clinical practice of nursing
  - › Your job
  - › Having a life
  - › The leadership skills of your immediate supervisor
  - › Your programming

<u>The two methods to prevent burnout</u>

1. Lower your stress levels and the drain they cause.
2. Increase your ability to recharge your energy accounts.

<u>The two responsible parties in our prevention efforts:</u>

1. The individual nurse—that would be you.
2. Your organization—the entity that is responsible for the workplace conditions of your current job.

Put these together, and you create a classic 2X2 matrix that will organize the tools in this chapter.

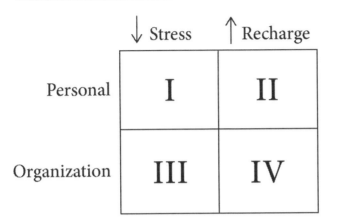

The Burnout Prevention Matrix

	↓ Stress	↑ Recharge
Personal	I	II
Organization	III	IV

In this chapter, you will learn several of the most powerful matrix tools in detail.

All of the tools are field-tested and nurse-approved through my own life and the lives and practices of hundreds of nurses I have worked with across the country. They are a selection of the first and most powerful burnout prevention techniques I teach.

Our focus will be on the things for which you can take complete responsibility.

These are new levels of awareness and new activities that you can put into place on your own. None of them require the approval of your supervisor, a budget, or the assistance of your IT department—thank heavens.

I suggest you read through the rest of this chapter as an overview first.

- Look at all the tools from each of the four quadrants.
- Take notes in your journal.
- Notice which tools fit into your Master Plan of changes you want to make to your current role.
- Read the ACTION STEPS for your selected tools at the end of their sections to start practicing them.

- Get ready to choose a tool and spin up your first plate in your next strategy session.

One last bit of head trash to take out

Before you move on to the tools, we have one more piece of head trash to isolate and remove.

You are going to be learning and practicing new skills in the pages ahead. You are a beginner here, and there is an important first lesson to learn.

Complete the following statement:

"Practice makes _____."

If you answered with the word "perfect," I want you to know that is a piece of head trash. Every time a person hears this three word sentence, a little voice in their head goes off simultaneously, *I will never be perfect, so why should I practice?*

"Practice makes perfect" is actually a non-supportive thought. It comes from your perfectionist programming, and it will block your impulse to do the work of practicing any new skill. Yet, practice is absolutely essential for a simple reason:

Practice makes *better.*

Remember this when you are practicing the new skills below. Remember it from now on whenever you are helping your patients, your team, your children, or your significant other learn something new.

Practice makes better.

Practice with this mindset. Learn to live your life from this new perspective and see what a difference it makes.

Fill in the blank:

Practice Makes _____

QUADRANT I: PERSONAL STRESS RELIEF

"A real decision is measured by the fact that you've taken a new action.
If there's no action, you haven't truly decided."
—Tony Robbins

"Many of us feel stress and get overwhelmed not because we're taking on too much, but
because we're taking on too little of what really strengthens us."
—Marcus Buckingham

ELECTRONIC MEDICAL RECORDS (EMR) AND DOCUMENTATION

IN RECENT SURVEYS of nurse stress factors, electronic charting always makes the list. The hassles of documentation can get in the way of being present with the patient and block you from any semblance of a healing patient encounter. It is not uncommon for nurses to spend hours after their shift charting in the EMR and additional hours—outside of clinical work—in class learning how to use new systems and monitor updates. We often feel that the time spent documenting keeps us away from the thing we do best as nurses: spending time with the patient.

EMR is also one of the most common aspect of clinical practice where nurses feel out of control and overwhelmed, yearn for a magic pill solution, or wish it would just go away.

These symptoms among nurses should be a head trash clue for you at this point. As you read this sentence, imagine a flashing red light leaping from the page and a claxon screaming,

"DILEMMA ALERT … DILEMMA ALERT …"

Remember our discussion of problems vs. dilemmas back in Chapter 2?

EMR is not a problem. EMR is another dilemma.

Much of nursing's suffering around EMR is because it is not a problem, no matter how much we would like it to be. Before I help you shape your strategy to address EMR, here are the most important things to know about it.

EMR is not going away—no matter how much you might wish it would. It is here to stay. You either learn to be as much of an expert in the software as you can—or commit to regular training and education in its use—or you will suffer and get home later than needed.

There is no "solution" for EMR and the requirements of documentation. This is not because it is impossible to address. It is because EMR is *not a problem*. You can stop trying to solve it or wishing it would disappear.

EMR is a true blue dilemma.

If you want to minimize its effect on your quality of life and get home sooner, your job is to build a simple EMR strategy - three to five new actions you will turn into your new EMR habits going forward.

The two horns

I believe the best expression of the two horns of the EMR dilemma is Documentation vs. Time with the Patient (time at the bedside). The balance point you seek is adequate documentation with the minimum input of effort so you can spend more time at the bedside.

Let me show you some proven components of an EMR strategy here. It is up to you to pick just one of the options below, put it into use, and make it a new documentation habit. Remember plate spinning and the one-at-a-time method of implementation of your action steps. Remember, too, that this is a strategy. It will ultimately have multiple parts.

EMR strategy components

1.) Check Your Attitude

Often, one of the biggest problems with EMR is our basic attitude toward the technology. Many nurses feel this way when they think about their EMR program. *Every line of the code of this EMR was written by the devil himself, in the fires of hell, and whenever I am at the keyboard, he is digging his fingernails into the backs of my hands.*

Just so you know, this attitude is called "being a hater." It is extremely common and, unfortunately, is the source of much suffering around documentation.

Let me ask you this: Do you really think EMR is just a fad and it will go away in a year or two? How does being a hater help you get home sooner? You will recognize complaining and blaming as signs you are playing the role of the victim. Remember, this is just head trash.

When we fail to embrace the technology, we never learn how to use it well. Every time you touch the keyboard, your attitude changes, and hassles seem to sprout like weeds in a garden.

Don't be a hater.

Hating the EMR is an emotion that gets in the way of completing your documentation efficiently.

Here is a place where I am very sympathetic with your situation. I understand how painful it can be to chart every two hours on pain scores, only to have to go back into the electronic record to document whether the interventions given had any effect. It can be extremely tedious and time-consuming to have to check every patient's orders several times a day. And when changes are made to the patient's EMR without our knowledge, we can become completely infuriated.

EMR is painful, exhausting, frustrating, maddening, and more.

My sympathy, empathy, and compassion does absolutely no good unless—and until—you step away from playing the victim. Victims don't get better at documentation. Victims blame, justify, and complain while nothing around them changes.

EMR is here to stay. If you don't embrace it and learn to be an expert at it, you are only guaranteeing your misery and struggles will continue.

There are ways to improve your skills, set up better systems to organize your workflow, and use your IT support teams more efficiently. When you notice negative emotions come up around charting, take a big breath and release them. Check your attitude and take the step below.

Commit to becoming a power user

I encourage you to commit to becoming a power user of your specific EMR system. If your organization is not already documenting electronically, volunteer to participate in the decision-making, design, testing, and evaluation of documentation processes and information systems as they are set up. Do everything you can to become an expert in the operation of the EMR program at your job.

Here are some steps that work in the real world.

a.) Take all the training your IT support team gives you—twice.

Make sure your colleagues, support staff, and providers do too. Learn everything there is to learn from the trainings offered, and realize that is just a basic foundation.

b.) Use the full capabilities of the software.

Believe it or not, EMR programs were designed with the intention to make documentation easier. Unfortunately, most were not designed by working nurses. However, all of them have features that allow you to set up personalized charting screens and customized ways to view your orders.

As a power user, you will want to squeeze the juice out of every single ounce of the customization options for your software so that it matches your personal workflow.

Here is the acid test for your documentation. Answer this question:

If you look back over last week's shifts, what percentage of your shifts did you have to stay late at work to complete your charting?

You are doing very well if your answer is 30 percent or less. If you find yourself in front of the computer charting all shift long (and constantly staying late to finish up your documentation), there are massive time savings available to you from using the customizable functions inside your system.

- Screen configurations
- Quick keys / Smart phrases
- Any type of templated organizational component within the system's capability

Take the time to set up your own templates so you can create systems to organize your workflow.

While it can feel like you are spending most of your shift in front of a computer, studies show that, in reality, this is not the case.[8] Be gentle with yourself as you become efficient with electronic charting.

c.) Study the native power users on your team.

- Who are the people on your unit who do not complain about the EMR?
- Who are the doctors, nurses, or receptionists who get home on time with their work done and love the program—the ones everyone acknowledges are good at it, the ones who would never go back to your old charting method?
- NOTE: These power users may be hiding in your organization. It is often unpopular to say you like the EMR out loud. You may have to dig a little to find them.

Ask them if you can watch how they chart.

They always say, "Yes." Arrange a time when you can sit next to them while they are at their computer. Sit just over their shoulder and lean in the way an umpire in the major leagues leans on the back of the catcher. Watch exactly what they do when they are charting. If that means you accompany them into their patient's room, so be it.

There will come a moment when you suddenly tell them to stop as they do a quick set of keystrokes, charting on a PRN medication in a millisecond. Stop them whenever you need them to stop. Have them show you exactly what they just did to make that note appear out of nowhere. Don't ask them what their favorite shortcuts are. You probably wouldn't understand their explanation. Instead, have them show you *exactly* what they do when they are charting. Take notes. Learn their shortcuts by watching what they do in their practice.

Ask to borrow their templates for customized screen configurations and note templates.

These are the people who have the most useful and organized charting setup of anyone in your group. They are always just fine with sharing. It is no work on their part to show you their templates. In fact, I have never heard of a power user refusing this request.

Now that you have watched them working the EMR and have their templates, do what they do, the way they do it, and keep tweaking this foundation to match your personal workflow even more effectively.

Just one tip from a power user colleague can make a huge difference in each patient encounter when you are completing your documentation. Saving a couple minutes on every PRN medication from this day forward will eventually add up to major time-saving for you. When you release the hater, learn some power user tips, and dedicate yourself to improving your documentation skills, these little changes can add up to major time savings. The time you save in documentation can be devoted to what you love to do instead ... taking care of your patients and their families.

Remember, you only have to set up your customizable workflow once. Each template, quick key, smart phrase, or other automated chart entry you put into play is a permanent upgrade in your documentation skills. You benefit from the organized charting system forever.

Even if your workplace changes the EMR system at some point, don't panic. It is usually a simple process to transfer your current workflow automation components to the new system.

2.) Chart Only What is Required—the Organizational Policies.

Last, but not least, it is very important to recognize and release your perfectionist programming. Most nurses who really struggle with charting are being driven by their perfectionist programming to document the patient's status, what they did, the outcome, and new or continuing plans for care in beautiful prose every time. These nurses write beautiful, flowing, full sentences with perfect spelling and punctuation in each patient's chart every day. I strongly encourage you to stop that now.

A free text narrative is not the Great American Novel.

Punctuation, sentence structure, and grammar are irrelevant. Ask yourself, *What are the purposes of a free text narrative?* Document only enough to fulfill those purposes. In fact, there is a reason the EMR is set up the way it is: to move us away from free text narratives. Here are three reasons to minimize your use of free text notes.

The three reasons to avoid free text narratives

a.) Nobody reads them.

Sure, the check boxes and drop down menus can make documentation feel very robotic. However, these screens—when set up correctly—are actually designed to make the work go quicker.

A study published in *The Journal of the American Medical Informatics Association*[9] reported that users of EMR spent 20 to 103 minutes per day authoring notes and 7 to 56 minutes per day viewing notes. In fact, they found that only about 20 percent of nurses' notes are read by anyone, ever.

B.) It makes it easier to use the data.

When free text narratives are written, data auditors actually have to go through manually to search narrative fields for the desired information. When electronic charting is entered into discrete fields, the data can be aggregated, sorted, and manipulated easier for reporting outcomes and conducting research. If your EMR does not allow comments or free text narratives, this is likely on purpose. These options are being deliberately left out so the data can be used in a more meaningful way.

C.) It is part of the policy.

Many nurses have expressed concern about how "charting to exception" is inadequate. However, as nurses, we know we were trained to follow our organizational policies and procedures. If your organizational policy supports charting by exception, then it does meet the legal standard of care for nursing documentation.[10]

This concept of charting to the exception underlies all of the other recommendations above. It is something to keep in mind at all times. As Joyce Sensmeier, MS RN, Vice President of Informatics at HIMSS (Health Information Management Systems Society) says, "We have to get past documenting that way and move to outcomes. We need to show the impact of nursing care—the patient improving or not being readmitted because of what the nurse does."[11]

3.) Use Your Team

Once you are on the path to becoming a power user, don't forget you have a team here.

I encourage you to rise above your Lone Ranger programming and utilize all the brainstorming power of your colleagues and coworkers. Gather your administrative coordinator, fellow nurses, and support staff (or anyone who is involved in your patient flow or chart entries) and get everyone's ideas on how to optimize the process of electronic charting.

Here, you need to ask powerful, open-ended questions that start with the words *what* or *how*. Here are some examples:

- What do you see me doing that I can stop—or you can do better?
- What ideas do you have on how we can make documentation easier?
- How can we share the charting activities more effectively?

In most cases, your team has important ideas they have not shared with you simply because you haven't asked for their input.

Make a list of their ideas, prioritize the suggestions, and pick one to implement together. You will be surprised at the power of the action plans you can create when you bring your team in on documentation struggles early and often. Just remember to implement one improvement at a time.

4.) Bring Your Computer into the Room

Often, nurses feel they don't have enough nearly time with their patients. When we are glued to a computer, it's impossible to make the human connections we all crave. Many of us went into nursing to help patients heal. How can we do that if we're stuck behind a screen all day?

A powerful way to carve out more face-to-face time with your patients is to stop separating patient care and documentation. If at all possible, bring your computer into the patient's room and do your charting at the bedside with the patient. If you use a laptop or tablet, carry it to the bedside. Use a C.O.W (computer on wheels) or a W.O.W. (workstation on wheels) to bring your charting to the patient.

As you go through your patient assessment, take short breaks to chart as you go. Just let the patient know when you switch from focusing on them to focusing on the chart.

You might say something simple like, "Okay, now I am going to enter what we just discussed in the chart. I will be right back." When you are done charting and ready to focus back on the patient, just let them know with a quick, "All right, I am back. What is it we were just discussing?"

It is important to tell the patient and their family members when you change your focus from them to the chart and back again. Simple phrases like the ones above, spoken as you look them in the eyes and perhaps a touch of their hands, will make this a natural, flowing process.

Patient care and charting, simultaneously and in the same room, will reduce your time spent with the computer while increasing your patient's satisfaction with your care. You get to spend more time with the patient and the charting gets done at the same time.

What about the charting that happens minute-by-minute throughout the day? Same thing. If you give patients a PRN medication and want to reassess their pain after the fact, ask them at the bedside, and when they respond, enter their new pain rating right into your notes.

Don't Do This

Please do not just walk into your patient's room, computer in arm, and start firing questions at them without making eye contact. This will feel rushed and rude. Even when you document your charting at the patient's bedside, be sure to make that personal connection first. Be sure to make eye contact. Let the patient speak. Really listen to what he or she is saying. Ask clarifying questions in an open-ended fashion that provides the patient with opportunity to speak.

All the while, chart as you go so you don't have to remember everything and spend hours after work getting it all down into the EMR later.

In fact, this is how the National Nurse's Week virtual conference was born. Nurses from across the country were telling me how "click and pick" nursing was getting in the way of human connection and patient care. For more information on how to bring this art of nursing back into your professional practice, check out the Art of Nursing program here:

www.ElizabethScala.com/

Our twelve-nurse faculty all spoke on ways to be more present with our patients as we navigate the electronic medical record and online documentation systems.

An EMR strategy monitoring system

Here are some metrics I suggest you consider using to monitor the effectiveness of your EMR strategy:

- The average amount of time between giving your handoff report and leaving the workplace.
- The number of times you have to go back into a patient's record and re-enter documentation from your first assessment of the day. Tell your perfectionist programming to give you a break when this happens.
- The amount of time you spend charting while on break. Again, you may need to do this from time to time, no matter what. Perfectionist be gone!

EMR/DOCUMENTATION SUMMARY

1. EMR is a dilemma.
2. You are looking to build an EMR strategy.
3. Suggested EMR strategy steps

   Don't be a hater. Become a power user instead.
   Chart Only What is Required—the Organizational Policies.
   Use your team.
   Bring your computer into the room.

EMR/Documentation ACTION STEPS

NOTE: The plate spinning theory applies here. These are components of an EMR strategy that will work. Take them one at a time.

- Check your attitude when using the EMR. Consider giving up any negative thoughts or feelings to the Squeegee Breath (which we'll discuss in the next section) so they don't slow you down.

- Consider using one of the steps in your charting routine as a trigger for your Squeegee Breath. (See "Mindfulness-Based Stress Relief (MBSR) and the Squeegee Breath" in the next section.)
- Take a look at your current charting practices. How can you reorganize them to make your workflow more efficient?
- When can you request and review the training available for your EMR system?
- Who are the native power users in your group?
- When will you schedule a power user observation session?
- Prioritize, select, and implement a team documentation activity.
- If you do not currently chart at the bedside, how can you make that happen?
- Journal on your experiences.

MINDFULNESS-BASED STRESS RELIEF (MBSR) AND THE SQUEEGEE BREATH

"Mindfulness is simply being aware of what is happening right now without wish-ing it were different; enjoying the pleasant without holding on when it changes (which it will); being with the unpleasant without fearing it will always be this way (which it won't)."
—James Baraz

"The best way to capture moments is to pay attention. This is how we cultivate mind-fulness. Mindfulness means being awake. It means knowing what you are doing."
—Jon Kabat-Zinn

MINDFULNESS-BASED STRESS RELIEF teaches you how to monitor and optimize "who you are being" at work.

With an effective mindfulness practice, you can become the "eye of the storm" in your workday—calm and centered no matter what is going on around you. This is not positive psychology or thinking happy thoughts. Mindfulness is a powerful, proven stress-relief tool for nurses. It has a history of stress-relieving effects that go back thousands of years.

Jon Kabat-Zinn

The use of mindfulness as a tool in healthcare in the US begins with Jon Kabat-Zinn and his founding of the Center for Mindfulness in Medicine, Health Care, and Society at the University of Massachusetts in 1979.

Kabat-Zinn was a student of the Vietnamese Buddhist monk Thích Nhất Hạnh, from whom he learned *vipassanā*, or mindfulness meditation. He originally taught meditation, simple yoga poses, and body scan imagery to patients in the UMass healthcare system with intractable mental and physical diseases. Mindfulness was so effective in symptom relief across such a broad range of illnesses that soon the doctors began to attend classes alongside their patients.

The physicians noticed they learned to become calmer, more centered, and more focused in their practices as a result of learning to meditate.

Multiple studies replicating Kabat-Zinn's program have shown significant stress relief effects for physicians in the last thirty years. Today, Mindfulness-Based Stress Relief (MBSR) is acknowledged as the most researched and effective burnout prevention tool for both physicians and nurses.

What is mindfulness?

The simplest and most accurate description of the state of mindfulness is this: *being present to what is happening here and now; releasing thoughts and feelings that keep you from this present moment without judgment.*

Mindfulness means giving whatever is in front of you right now *your undivided attention.*

Here is why this is such a powerful stress-relieving and illness-modifying skill. Notice how often your mind wanders to topics that are not in front of you here and now, especially when you are in the flow of your workday.

It is extremely common for our thoughts to be dominated by:

- Worrying about things you did and patients you assessed earlier in the day (the past).
- Thinking about things on your to-do list that you haven't gotten to yet—or medications you will be giving out later today - or what you have to do after work, like pick up the children or make dinner (the future).
- Fear that something bad that happened in the past is going to happen again in the future (projection).
- Those funny random thoughts that come up in daydreams or distractions.

All of these thought patterns are normal, constant, and interfere with you giving *this* patient or *this* task your undivided attention in *this* moment. The distractions from being present are not just at work either. You are just as likely to be distracted when you are with your spouse or significant other or children when you are away from the unit.

For example: how often do you find yourself sitting at home thinking about work? This a very common form of distraction and "non-presence" for nurses.

When your awareness is dominated by worrying about the past or future, you are not able to relax into the present. It is stressful, even though we often don't even realize it is going on. The distraction of our consciousness causes a near-constant trickle of stress and energy leakage.

Mindfulness can stop the worry and the drain distraction causes, allowing you to be present, focused, and relaxed as you address the task at hand.

<u>Mindfulness is a skill set you use to:</u>

- **NOTICE** you are not present—that your thoughts and feelings are distracted.
- **RELEASE** those thoughts and feelings without judging yourself for having them.
- **RETURN** your undivided attention to the present and the task at hand.

<u>NOTICE > RELEASE > RETURN</u>

<u>Why is mindfulness important?</u>

Your ability to be fully present and focus your undivided attention on the person or task in front of you is the key to a number of very important components of career and life satisfaction.

<u>Mindfulness is a core skill of:</u>

- Leadership
- Quality care and patient satisfaction—mindfulness is the essence of the healing encounter
- Parenting
- Love and caring for another
- Focus and attention to detail
- "Flow"—when you become completely absorbed in an activity to the point where time passes without you noticing
- Your ability to respond to an emergency situation such as a code

Mindfulness is such a foundational skill for the art of being a nurse, leader, spouse, and parent that I find it strange it is almost never taught to nurses until *after* they are suffering from burnout.

<u>The fast track to mindfulness</u>

Jon Kabat-Zinn taught meditation as a mindfulness tool, because that is how he learned it from Thích Nhất Hạnh. His training requires hours of weekly seated and walking meditation and a silent meditation retreat as your graduation from the program. This significant time commitment is the biggest impediment to wide adoption by nurses. Most nurses feel they are just too busy to take the time to develop a formal meditation practice.

Since he started the Center for Mindfulness, most studies of MBSR simply copied his training with different participant groups. We won't be doing that here. It is important to realize that *meditation is only one of many paths to practice mindfulness*. It is the way a Buddhist monk learns and teaches, but it is not the *only way* to cultivate your undivided attention.

Another drawback to formal meditation practice as a mindfulness tool is its abstraction from the workplace. The term "formal meditation" means carving a specific time out of the normal routine of your day to meditate. Then, you sit in silence in a special environment with special cushions, far from the physical environment and stresses of your nursing career.

You are practicing mindfulness in the absence of the stresses and distractions you hope it will help you address. Kabat-Zinn and other researchers have proven that meditation away from the workplace is effective in lowering stress, but why not start with a tool you can use when you need it most?

How about a mindfulness tool you can use inside the flow of your workday—something you can do at work to return to the present while you are hip deep in the distractions of your career?

Enter the "Squeegee Breath"

The Squeegee Breath is a four-part super-breath that can be incorporated seamlessly into any nurse's workday. You can learn the technique in five minutes and begin to use and benefit from it immediately. You will be learning and using it in your career here in just a minute or two.

This is the first burnout prevention tool I teach every nurse.

It is the key step to ending the downward spiral because it is about who you are being. You can release the stress around you and use your ability to be present as a barrier to further energy loss. You don't need anyone else's approval or permission. You can get started with the Squeegee Breath immediately while we plan the changes in your career that will take more time to implement.

You can do this

Before we begin, let me reassure you—you already know how to do this. The Squeegee Breath builds on what I call "native human mindfulness behavior."

Remember the last time you were standing in the hallway of your unit. The patient's door was closed in front of you, and you knew "Jane Doe" was on the other side. There is a Jane Doe on every unit. She is the patient you know is going to be a handful, just like always. You have probably been thinking about her ever since you saw her name on the schedule earlier in the day. You have reviewed her orders and medication list, and now it's time to open the door and get started.

As you put your hand on the doorknob, you pause. What do you do before you enter the room?

Right. You take a deep breath.

Why?

Right again. You are centering yourself so you are fully present and ready for anything. After all, we are talking about Jane Doe here.

That is native human mindfulness behavior. In this example, you take the breath without being aware of your intention. The Squeegee Breath transforms this normal behavior into a four-part super-breath you use with the conscious intention of focusing your awareness in the present.

Why "Squeegee?"

Think about the way you experience your reality under normal circumstances. Your awareness, operating through your senses, creates a window to the outside world. When you are preoccupied by thoughts and feelings, the distraction interferes with your ability to be present. It is as if your window to the world has become smudged and cloudy. You can't even see what is right in front of you clearly. You need an awareness window washer. You need a squeegee.

Have you ever seen a professional window washer cleaning the big windows on storefronts in your town? They have a wand covered with soap and water in one hand. They use the wand to scrub the window. In the other hand they have a squeegee. With a single swipe of the squeegee, the window is squeaky clean, so clear it is difficult to see there is a pane of glass in front of you.

Let me show you how to use a "Squeegee Breath" to clean the window of your awareness, release any thoughts or feelings that don't need to be here right now, and become calm, centered, and present. This is a single-breath method to give any object, person, or task your undivided attention.

The Squeegee Breath in four steps

Let's take a first walk through the four steps of the Squeegee Breath. Feel free to practice each step as you read it.

1.) Set Your Intention

Set the intention that you are going to release anything that does not need to be here at this point in time and become calm, relaxed, and completely present.

2.) Breathe In

Take a big breath in, all the way up to the top of your head.

Hold that breath in for a count of … two … three …

3.) Breathe Out and Release

Release and exhale all the way to the bottom of your feet. As this out breath moves from your head to your toes, feel the squeegee passing down the window of your awareness. You can release any distracting or non-supportive thought to this cleansing breath. Let the squeegee wipe you clean.

As you reach the bottom of that breath, hold it out for a count of … two … three …

4.) Smile

Let your breathing resume itself.

Smile and say "ahh."

Now it's your turn

If you were just reading the words above on this first time through, it's time to practice. Remember Einstein's definition of insanity—you have to take different actions if you want different results in your life. Here is another chance to do just that. I encourage you to stand up for your first couple Squeegee Breaths so you really get that sense of being wiped clean on the exhale.

Please stand up.

1. **Intention:** set your intention to release and become present.
2. **Breathe In:** inhale to the top of your head. Hold it in … two … three …
3. **Breathe Out:** exhale to the bottoms of your feet. Release. Give it all up to the squeegee. Hold it out … two … three …

4. **Smile:** resume your normal breathing pattern. Smile. Say "ahh."

Feels good, doesn't it? Here's the thing about the Squeegee Breath.

It works every time you use it.

When I say it works, I mean you will be calmer, more relaxed, and more present after you take a Squeegee Breath than if you did not take one.

How the Squeegee Breath works

The four parts of the Squeegee Breath combine to give you an authentic super-breath. It is a highly concentrated mini-meditation.

- Your intention is the most important part. Your desire to release and become present—and your intention that this next breath will provide that experience for you—is key.
- Breathing from your head to your toes provides a full-body release. You will get better and better at actually breathing from your head to your toes as you practice.
- The image of the squeegee wiping you clean allows you to feel the release as you exhale.
- Smiling and saying "ahh" is a mini-reward and celebration of you taking good care of yourself.

You practice the Squeegee "In Situ"

Best of all, you do all this right in the middle of your workday, the exact time and place you need it the most. It is like taking a class in college where they give you the final exam on day one. Well, you just passed the final, and it all gets easier from here.

What to give up to the Squeegee Breath

Feel free to let go of any unsupportive or distracting thoughts. Anything that takes you away from what is in front of you right now is something you can give up to the squeegee.

You may have a little voice in your head saying something like, *this is pretty wild, Buddhist, tutti-fruitti, woo-woo, out there weirdness.* Or, your inner voice might be saying, *I hope I am doing it the right way.* If you want, you can let both of those thoughts go to the squeegee.

- Set your intention to let them go.

- Big breath to the top of your head ... two ... three ...
- Release to the bottoms of your feet ... two ... three ...
- Inhale. Smile. Say "ahh."

The Squeegee Breath is like kegel exercises

You may also hear your inner voice say, *There is no way I am doing this in front of my patients and staff.* You can give that up too.

Out in the real world, a Squeegee Breath is a lot like Kegel exercises. Someone would really have to be watching you closely to notice the change in your breathing, especially if you do it while you are washing your hands, walking down the hallway, or in the privacy of the break room.

So, there you have it. A field-tested, single-breath mindfulness technique you can put to use and benefit from immediately. In fact, you probably already have. With the four parts of the Squeegee Breath, you are always only a single breath away from being much calmer, more centered, and more present.

NOTE: The only way you are too busy for the Squeegee is if you are too busy to breathe.

When to take a Squeegee Breath

Let me green light you to do it PRN ... whenever you feel you need it. I only wish it was that easy. However, with nurses, waiting until you feel like you need to take a Squeegee Breath is always a spectacular failure for a simple reason: your conditioning.

You are highly conditioned to ignore your own stress, worry, and distraction levels. If you wait until you feel like you need the squeegee, it is nearly always too late.

The Squeegee Breath is most effective when it becomes a regular habit in your practice day. Here is a lesson in habit formation science from the Stanford Persuasive Technology Laboratory that will help you develop your own Squeegee Breath habit.

The head of the lab is a fascinating man named B. J. Fogg. He spends half his time researching how to motivate people to change their behavior and the other half working with the developers of cell phone applications to make them more addictive.

Let me teach you one of his core concepts. If you're interested in learning more about him and his work, his website is *www.bjfogg.com*.

Dr. Fogg says that to create a new habit, you need to possess three things at once.

1.) Ability

You have to know how to do the new thing you want to do. In this case, you know how to do the Squeegee Breath. There are no more steps, no advanced training, and nothing more to learn about how to perform the Squeegee Breath. All that remains is for you to practice it. You have the ability now and will only get more skilled with time because Practice Makes _____.[12]

2.) Motivation

I have to assume you are motivated to lower your stress levels and be more present with your patients, coworkers, and family. I assume you can see the benefits of being completely present with all three and giving them the benefit of your undivided attention. So, you have the motivation too.

3) A Trigger

All that is missing right now is a trigger. The trigger reminds you to take the action. You need a trigger to remind you to do the Squeegee Breath in your workday.

B.J. Fogg says the very best trigger is an existing habit. You trigger a new habit with an old one. See how this works?

Ideally, you choose a special type of existing habit he calls a Super Habit.

Super Habits are things you would never *not* do.

The best Super Habits are also things you do repeatedly in the day. That way, you trigger the Squeegee Breath multiple times a day, whether you feel like you need it or not. This allows you to be proactive and get ahead of the stresses in your career, rather than waiting to notice you are frustrated and distracted before taking action.

Now, here is one reason I love working with nurses - we have so many Super Habits to choose from. Answer this question for me:

What is something you do multiple times a day at work—perhaps between each patient—that you would never NOT do?

Think about it for a few seconds, and you will see the routine of your patient flow has dozens of Super Habits embedded within.

The most obvious one is hand washing. Others include opening the door, reviewing the chart, multiple different steps in the EMR, using the bathroom, sitting down to document, and many more.

All you have to do is pick one. Then, set the intention that you will use this Super

Habit as your Squeegee Breath trigger. Add in a simple way of tracking how often you take a Squeegee Breath in your day and you are nearly there.

I recommend you track your progress with a sticky note in a prominent place—one that you walk past regularly in your day. Put a pen or pencil tick mark every time you take a Squeegee Breath. Celebrate every one.

- Treat yourself like a dog.
- Keep track of your totals from day to day.
- Play games by rewarding yourself for reaching five or ten or a personal daily best.
- Feel free to switch out your Super Habit trigger if you find this one difficult.
- Play with different triggers until you hit on one that works for you.

You are now a Squeegee Breath teacher too.

You weren't aware until now that the last several pages were the Squeegee Breath train-the-trainer course as well. You are now also a fully-fledged Squeegee Breath trainer. I strongly encourage you to teach this single super-breath technique to your staff, your patients, and your family.

Here is an example of what you might do in your career.

Sharing the Squeegee

Let's say you walk into the patient's room and see that she is in pain or upset.

Notice it and say something like, "You look uncomfortable and upset. Let's take a big breath together and let some of that go."

Then, look her in the eye and breathe "squeegee style" with her as many times as you would like. You will see her relax and synchronize her breathing with yours—and probably smile and thank you with each breath.

That is all it takes. You don't have to say the word "squeegee" if you don't want to. I guarantee the patient will appreciate your caring and feel better after the breaths.

The same breath works just as well with your coworkers and especially with your children. Remember, you are a certified Squeegee Breath instructor now. Spread the benefits of mindfulness by simply teaching people how to breathe with intention.

SQUEEGEE BREATH SUMMARY

1. Mindfulness is noticing you are distracted, releasing the distracting thoughts

and feelings, and returning to give the present moment your *undivided attention.*

2. Squeegee Breath: Four Steps

> Intention: Set your intention to release and become present.

> Breathe In: Inhale to the top of your head. Hold it in … two … three …

> Breathe Out: Exhale to the bottoms of your feet. Release. Give it all up to the squeegee. Hold it out … two … three …

> Smile: Resume your normal breathing pattern. Smile. Say "ahh."

3. Use a Super Habit trigger to remind you to practice your Squeegee Breath during your workday.

Squeegee Breath ACTION STEPS

- What is your squeegee trigger?
- How will you track the number of Squeegee Breaths you take a day?
- How will you celebrate each breath?
- What is your reward for your first "10-Squeegee Day"?
- Who is the first person you want to teach the Squeegee Breath to?
- Journal on your experience.

BONUS:

Consider additional squeegee triggers such as:

- Red lights and stop signs
- The spinning ball or hourglass when your computer freezes

NOTE:

The Squeegee Breath is one component of an online video mindfulness program called One Minute Mindfulness, developed by my co-author Dike Drummond MD. This eight lesson training was proven effective in reducing stress and burnout and increasing mindfulness in a group of volunteer physicians. Here is the study reference: EXPLORE January/February2016,Vol.12,No.1

The techniques are completely effective in nurses too. Learn more about the training here:

http://www.thehappymd.com/mbsr-one-minute-mindfulness-for-physicians

THE BID TEAM HUDDLE

The Squeegee Breath is classic resilience training. It is about making a change in who you are being at work, rather than changing the work itself. The Squeegee Breath is the first tool I teach my coaching clients because it has the miraculous effect of eliminating suffering right off the bat. When you can let go of frustration, overwhelm, and anxiety with a single breath, your days become much less stressful and you leak less energy right away. And resilience is never enough all by itself.

The next several tools, starting here with the BID Team Huddle, will change the structures and systems of your work day to permanently eliminate stress. This allows you to combine changes in who you are being with a change in what you are doing for an additional drop in the energy drain of being a nurse.

Team huddle power training

After regular use of the Squeegee Breath, a well-done BID Huddle with your nursing team is the single most powerful stress reduction technique for nurses. It amazes me how many nurses skip a team huddle because they are *too busy*. I believe the reason is because it is very easy to do a team huddle poorly. Let me show you what I call *Team Huddle Power Training* so you can learn how to use a three-minute huddle to save you forty-five minutes a day.

You are most likely familiar with the concept of a team huddle. You may have even tried it and seen it be only temporarily effective. The most common reason for a huddle having only a temporary effect is the leader stops calling the huddle after a while. Whether you work in the hospital and your huddles are led by your nurse manager or charge nurse, or you work in an outpatient setting where the physician calls the huddle, too often it is only a passing fad rather than a solid team habit and a core component of your burnout prevention strategy.

This happens for a simple reason. *Survival mode and a team huddle are incompatible with each other.*

It is easy to feel like you are too busy to take time for the huddle. There seems to be so much to do that the only logical action is to dive right into the chaos of your day and start checking orders and medications. "We don't have time to huddle; there are patients in rooms."

This is a huge missed opportunity to de-stress your day.

Your team huddle is an investment in a smooth workday. Every minute in a well-run huddle will save you a minimum of five later on and dramatically lower the stress level for you and your team members by putting out fires before they start.

Why BID

Most things in healthcare revolve around relatively predictable chunks of time.

In the hospital, physicians often come onto the hospital unit, round on patients, and make changes to the orders in the mornings and evenings. Your charge nurse, rounding nurse, or discharge navigator who attended rounds reports off to the nursing staff of any changes made to the orders, often in the middle of the day or shift.

In an outpatient clinic, the most common schedule is to see patients in the mornings and afternoons with a mid-day break.

In each setting, a huddle at the start of the day or shift and a regrouping huddle in the middle of the day or shift often provides the maximum efficiency boost.

A hospital example:

You get to work for an AM shift. You receive morning report from the off-going nurses. The day shift charge nurse calls all of the nursing staff to the breakroom to review patient assignments. Later in the day, after patient rounds are over, the charge nurse brings everyone back to the team room for a short midday huddle to review discharges, patient transfers, admissions, and any staffing concerns.

An outpatient example:

You arrive in the office at 7:30 a.m. with the first patient scheduled at eight. At 7:45 a.m., your doctor calls the huddle where you, the doctor, the receptionist and any other members of the care team review and troubleshoot the schedule for the AM. At midday, you huddle again to assign tasks left over from the AM and preview and troubleshoot the PM schedule.

The basic team huddle process

- Make time for the huddle—just three minutes before exiting the team room to start back into the workday. However, it must be blocked out and a part of everyone's daily workflow and be scheduled to start before you begin your patient care responsibilities. Remember, this is an investment in everyone's peace of mind.

- Grab your schedule for the shift coming up—paper or electronic.
- Huddle up with all the members of your team.
  - Hospital: Charge nurse, nursing staff, clinical technicians, customer service coordinators … anyone who is on the schedule and working with nursing staff for the upcoming shift.
  - Outpatient: Receptionists, nurses, MA's, onsite lab techs, physician, Nurse-Practitioner, Physician's Assistant
- Run through the schedule.
  - Which patient has special needs or should be in a special room?
  - Which one is upset, angry, or really sick?
  - What open rooms are available on the unit, and what patients are slotted for admissions? Or, what appointment slots are available and what rules will you use to fill them?
- Add anything any member of the team wants to share with or request from the other team members to help patient flow go more smoothly.

That is as far as most people take the process of a team huddle. It can be so much more. Here are the power-training points I encourage you to incorporate in your huddles.

Team huddle power points

1.) Do this on every shift with all staff.

This will not work if only some of the nursing staff are doing them. If you have a huddle on Monday and Tuesday and no one else huddles in the rest of the week, it becomes very difficult to sustain. That pattern is what a team huddle looks like as it is sputtering into oblivion. Remember, you are creating a *burnout prevention strategy* here. This new action must become a regular habit to be effective. It must become "the way we do things around here." Ideally, this becomes a team effort with the entire nursing staff and other staff members on board.

2.) Make a human connection.

Use the huddle as an opportunity to check in with the team at a deeper level. Ask how everyone is doing. Make sure you know whose birthday it is, who is pregnant, whose child just made honor roll, who is doing well, and who is stressed today. The huddle is an important opportunity for a quick person-to-person check in. Don't miss it.

3.) Squeegee in and out.

I strongly recommend you start and end the huddle with a Squeegee Breath. You might start the huddle with something like, "Hey, everyone, let's take a big breath and get really present here in the huddle." (In to the top … two … three … Out to the feet … two … three. Ahh.)

Complete the huddle and finish with, "Hey everyone, let's do one more of those big breaths and let it all go before we head out."

Remember, you are a certified Squeegee Breath trainer. It can be that simple, and I guarantee everyone will appreciate it.

4.) Delegate responsibility for the huddle.

The reason the BID Huddle is not universal is simple: nurses and doctors are rushed and want to get on with their shifts. We get too busy. We take a look at the schedule and can't resist diving right in. Our workaholic, Lone Ranger programming takes over and we dive into the pile of tasks with complete disregard for the team.

The huddle will often last only a week or two if you let the senior nurse (hospital) or physician (outpatient) be the one who calls the huddle together.

The solution is to delegate the calling of the huddle to someone other than the nurse manager of the unit or the physician in an outpatient setting. Pick a Huddle Champion. They call the huddle and run the steps. If you decide to do this, remember to give your Huddle Champion permission to gently force all the members of the huddle—physicians, nurses, and staff - to attend when they try skip out of the huddle down the road. We know the urge to skip the huddle will get intense in the future, especially on busy days. Give your Huddle Champion permission now to call you out on the urge to skip and huddle up anyway.

5.) Have some fun.

The huddle is a great place to sing happy birthday, give high fives, and even put your hands in the middle and make a noise at the end … "Yay Team!" You can do things like go around the circle and everyone says one word that sums up how they are feeling today. The sky's the limit on fun and creativity in your huddles.

BID Huddle ACTION STEPS

- Who is on your BID Huddle Team?
- When does it make sense to hold your huddles? (You can ask the team this question too. Let go of your Lone Ranger. When you find yourself struggling to answer a question, let them help you.)
- When will you tell your team and get started?
- What is one fun thing you would like to do in your huddles?
- Who could you delegate the BID Huddle to?
- When will you do that?
- Journal on your experience.

TEAM BUILDING

NURSES ARE A lot like superheroes in some ways. Out in the real world, if there is some type of emergency, the nurse in the crowd is the one who is going to step up and dive right in to help. We can't help but help out.

At the very same time, we often behave as though we are on a deserted island—needing to do it all alone. This is our Lone Ranger programming.

Superhero and Lone Ranger often seem like they are joined at the hip.

Think about it: have you ever been drowning during your shift—with documentation piling up and patients going south—but never asked for or accepted any help? What happens when the charge nurse or other colleague comes up to you in the hall and asks if you need a hand? You got it …

"No. I'm fine. Don't need anything right now."

I'm fine. Two little words with a huge impact. You continue on with your shift and wonder why you're staying three hours after it ends to get your charting done. Your day has extended itself for one simple reason: you are acting like a superhero Lone Ranger.

Sure, each time you say "I'm fine" may only cause you to lose four to five minutes each. Add it up, though, and you will get sixty to ninety minutes of wasted time in your day.

No other industry would allow that kind of inefficiency. Yet in medicine, it is every nurse for him or herself when it comes to asking for and receiving help. Your programming teaches you to avoid asking for help lest it be seen as a sign of weakness. You are not in training now and you are surrounded by a team. It is time to learn how to work together rather than each of us on our own individual gerbil wheel.

The solution is TEAM BUILDING

You don't have to do everything all by yourself. Nurses can learn to delegate, share the load, and ask for help. It is possible to learn these team building skills.

Tasks that are not nurse specific can be delegated to support staff. Nurses who have discharged their patients and are looking for something to do can be called upon to help those with tasks remaining.

Charge nurses who ask if you need help will rise to the occasion if you say, "Yes, please." And don't forget—we often have nurse managers, clinical nurse specialists, and nurse educators within our reach to help us out in a jam. We're nurses, right? You are always trying to lend a hand and your colleagues feel the same way. All we have to do is allow them—and invite them to support us.

Every time you accept help or help out a team member in need, you build the team's ability to share the load and have each other's backs. Every time you accept help or help out, you also make it normal to support your team mates … rather than have the team culture that asking for help is a sign of weakness.

Watch out for the superhero Lone Ranger here too

This behavior also comes into play around your work schedule—especially when you are asked to work extra shifts.

How many times have you been at home when the phone rang? You look at the caller ID and see that it is work calling. You cringe as you answer the phone, knowing it will be a fellow nurse on the other end of the line asking if you can work extra. And what do you do? Before you think twice, you hear yourself agreeing to come into work four hours early to help fill another staffing hole on your unit.

What can you do to lower your own stress and ensure that your time is actually your own?

TEAM BUILDING TOOLS

Tool #1: Find a work buddy

Create a buddy system in your workplace. Find a colleague to be your partner. Make a pact to have each other's back at work in ways that prevent overwhelm. "I will look out for you if you will look out for me." You can also point out situations where your work buddy says something like, "I'm fine" when they are actually overwhelmed. These observations can begin to break the superhero Lone Ranger programming cycle.

It's also a good idea to come up with a code word so when your work buddy sees your day spiraling out of control, she can come to you with non-judgmental and un-biased support. When she says, for example, "monkey," you know it's time to back off the superhero complex and allow her to step in and give you a hand.

Since you have agreed to be a team, receiving help from your work buddy doesn't create an immediate need for reciprocity. Sure, you'll help her out in the future—that's what the buddy system is for. However, just knowing there is someone who can help you when you need (and you'll do the same in return) makes it a little bit easier to accept the help when it is offered.

Tool #2: Build a Balance Sheet

One way to change the habit of constantly working overtime is to balance your "yes" and "no" responses. Here is a tool I use and teach to help you say "no" more often.

Pull out a blank sheet of paper. Across the top, write one thing you are struggling to say "no" to. In our case here, let's use the habit of saying "yes" when you are asked to help out when the staffing is short. So you might write "Extra shift requests" on the top of your paper in this case. This is the thing you are having trouble saying "no" to.

Use your pen to make two columns on the page. Label one column "Yes" and the other "No." This is your Balance Sheet. Here you will track just how often you say yes and no to this request. Every time work calls, grab this piece of paper. Refer to it as you respond to their request.

Okay, so the phone is ringing, and it's your workplace on the other line. You know as well as I do they didn't call you just to check in. As you go to pick up your phone, grab your Balance Sheet.

Sometimes, you will go in to work early to help out your unit. Who doesn't want to be a team player? In those cases, place a check mark in the "yes" column. At other times—especially when you see the "yes" column getting overridden with check marks—you will say "no."

You cannot be the only nurse on your team who comes in extra to work. Sometimes, you're just going to have to say "no." If you need to practice saying "no" ahead of time, ask your partner or spouse to help you out. Or, look in the mirror and rehearse until you are comfortable with saying, "No. I cannot come into work early today. I have plans."

Team-building is an integral part of surviving as a nurse.

You have to become comfortable with asking for and receiving help. You don't have to say "yes" all the time. If you are not able to rely on the other members of your team, it's no wonder you're stuck at work each night, finishing up on your charting hours after your shift is over.

Remember to ask your team for help.

You are never alone as a nurse. It is not your job to figure this out all on your own. Use your team. I know they want to help.

- Ask them for suggestions on creating the buddy system.
- Work together to implement it.
- Talk with your nurse manager about your workload and how you and your colleagues can assist each other.
- Thank them for their help and support. Treat them like dogs for sure.

Team building ACTION STEPS

- Who on your team would make a good work buddy?
- Which nurse can you partner up with so you have time to chart?
- Have a conversation with one of your colleagues to see if he or she would like to join you in working together on back-and-forth support.
- Make your yes/no Balance Sheet.
- Practice saying "no" aloud (either in private or with a trusted family member).
- The next time work calls you to come in for overtime, refer to your sheet and answer with confidence.
- Journal on your experience.

BROKEN RECORD AUTOMATION

DO YOU EVER feel like a broken record on your unit?

You know the old vinyl albums we played back in the day on a phonograph with a needle? Sometimes, they would skip and play the same thing over and over until you grabbed the needle and picked it up from the face of the spinning black disc. Do you ever feel like that during your week at work?

Do you find yourself saying the same thing over and over again to your patients?

Do you ever find yourself typing the same thing over and over into the EMR?

Every time you get stuck in this cycle, you likely get more and more frustrated with your charting (and the patients you've got to document on). The whole process becomes very tedious and time-consuming, and you are stuck … just like the needle on that old vinyl record.

Not only that, this "broken record" repetition can be a major source of stress because what you are doing doesn't even require the skills and experience of a nurse. You did not go to nursing school for this.

Rather than clench your jaw and growl the next time you feel like a broken record, let me encourage you to do something else instead.

Smile. Here's why …

This broken record feeling marks some of the quickest ways to optimize your shift, find more time to spend with your patients, and get home sooner. Don't get frustrated. Do this instead.

Broken record = automate & delegate

A broken-record moment is an opportunity to get your work done faster and more efficiently in a single step. You transform the broken record into better workflow by automating and/or delegating that repeated activity.

In my work with overstressed nurses, we have found the broken-record moments tend to occur in only two locations: patient education and documentation. Just think about your own experience right now. When do you say to yourself, "OMG, this is the twelfth time this week I have typed the same thing into the chart," or, "OMG, this is the seventh time I have taught a patient this treatment step?" Usually you notice the repetition and then get frustrated. You can let that go now because these broken-record moments are pure gold. They mark the quickest ways to get your work done more quickly.

The first action here is to simply write down your list of broken-record moments as they occur. When you notice a documentation step or patient education activity you are doing over and over and over again, add it to your list of broken-record moments. For now, just make the list. It may take you a week or more to notice them and build your complete list.

Once you have the list, divide them into patient education and documentation categories, and use the action steps below to automate or delegate them.

Automating documentation broken records

The single most important action to automate a documentation broken-record moment is to stop free typing and find another way to enter the information.

There may be a location in your EMR that is set up to automatically enter what you are typing in on the keyboard. Ask your power user friend, study the organizational policies on documentation, and reach out to your supervisor for their advice. If there is already an automated way to enter this information … find it and do it.

The second option is to create a template if free typing is the only solution. Your EMR system may have a format for templates with a snazzy name like "quick keys" or "smart phrases" or such. Your power user friend is the best person to ask about this. How do they document this piece of data that is a true broken-record moment for you? Your final resort is to make a note that documents your broken-record moment in Word or some other word-processing program, and simply copy and paste it into the chart in the appropriate location.

Either way, you have transformed something you used to free type multiple times a shift into a single click or keystroke. Instead of becoming frustrated when you notice the broken record and doing it anyway, you are now getting your work done more effectively and with less stress.

Three broken-record solutions for patient education

When you have your list of patient education broken-record moments in hand, pick just one, use this solution list to stop working so hard, and repeat that cycle.

1.) Handout System
Invest some time in creating a quality handout with the patient education information on it. Put some of your personality and your specific tips, tools, links to Internet

videos, and more in there. Print it on colored paper so your instructions stand out from the sheaf of other white papers your patients take home from every healthcare encounter, most of which have to do with insurance or billing.

Keep all of your patient education handouts in an accordion file near the nurses' station so it is a snap for you to find the one you want, and hand it to your patient as you do your assessment or start your discharge teaching.

2.) Engage Your Team and Your Patients

Now, I know as nurses we love the part of our job that involves patient teaching. And yes, if you have the time in your shift to do so, by all means do. However, there are likely other members on your team who also enjoy this type of thing. If all you need is for your patient to receive a handout on remembering the times to take their scheduled medications throughout the day, is there someone else on your support staff who can do this? Do you have a clinical technician on your team who just loves spending time teaching patients?

And here's another option you may not have considered: what about the patients? They certainly are members of the healthcare team, right? Is there a way to engage them in their own teaching in a way that is meaningful to them?

Let's revisit the patient who needs teaching on taking an evening medication. While you're speaking with this patient about discharge, you might ask them what they like to do around eight o'clock at night. And what if their response is to have a small glass of milk with one dessert cookie? Wouldn't it be easy for them to remember to pair their evening medication with this daily treat? Sometimes, the patient-teaching encounter is so obvious that it is overlooked when we're wracking our brains to help.

3.) Video Education

Shoot a video of you or your team delivering a primetime version of your patient education. Load your patient education videos onto your organization's patient education system or unit-based YouTube channel. When patient education is the next step in the patient flow, hand the patient the video player and start the video. Allow the patient to watch the video, and then check in with the patient in a couple of minutes to see if they have questions. You may also want to create a take-home handout to go with these videos.

If your team is comfortable making the videos public, you can also give patients a handout with a link to the video on YouTube so they can watch from their computers at home.

I've seen nursing units get extremely creative with this. Someone on the staff acts as a patient receiving the teaching while another nurse delivers the message. Common patient questions and concerns are brought up, and this interactive style of learning really engages your patients in a fun and creative way.

One at a time

The plate-spinning theory holds here as well. Don't let yourself get overwhelmed creating a huge library of patient education materials all at once. Just like the plate spinner, the best way is to take this project on one intervention at a time.

Make a list of your broken-record moments in patient education. Pick just one. Build your handout, video, or other automated teaching system and put it into play.

Each time you automate patient education for another disease or illness process, your day just got shorter.

If you put some personality and solid information into your materials, they will do a better job of education than you talking off the cuff on a busy day for the sixth time about the same issue.

Broken-Record ACTION STEPS

- What are the situations where you most frequently feel like a broken record?
- When will you make your list of broken-record moments?
- What documentation broken-record moment would you like to address first?
- What technology would you like to use to teach your patients?
- Which patient education broken-record moment would you like to take on first?
- What is the first step to get started?
- Who on your team can help? (Don't forget about the patient as an integral team member!)
- Journal on your experience.

QUADRANT II: PERSONAL RECHARGE

"There's no such thing as work-life balance. There are work-life choices, and you make them, and they have consequences."
—Jack Welch

"Happiness is not a matter of intensity but of balance, order, rhythm, and harmony."
—Thomas Merton

NOW, WE SHIFT focus from relieving stress to enabling more effective recharge when you are off work. Most of these tools are focused on creating more life balance. Before I show you how to create work balance between your career and your larger life, I can't help but be distracted by yet another flashing red light and screaming siren trying to get our attention dead ahead. Are you noticing it too? Wait a minute, the red light is spelling something out now. It says …

DILEMMA ALERT … DILEMMA ALERT …

That's right—work-life balance is not a problem, either.

There is no simple, one-step solution to work-life balance. This is not because it is impossible to address, but because work-life balance is not a problem.

<u>Work-life balance is another dilemma.</u>

Let's stop looking for a solution, rise up and out of victim mode, and get going on the tasks to address a dilemma.

1. **DEFINE** the two horns of the dilemma and the optimum balance point.
2. Design a **STRATEGY** to create the balance you seek.
3. Build a **SYSTEM** to monitor the effectiveness of your strategy.
4. **TWEAK** your strategy and your system as often as needed.

Work-life balance is something you must attend to regularly using a multi-part strategy—three to five tools you will turn into new habits. These new actions, applied regularly, are the only way out of Einstein's Insanity Trap. If you are not paying attention to your work-life balance at least twice a month, your life will be out of whack very soon.

The two horns of the dilemma are clearly visible this time. Our job is to create a balancing act out of what is typically a battle.

Work vs. Life

The balance point you seek is the time and energy devoted to each. You feel you are doing a good job and making enough money at work *and* your life outside of work is fulfilling and well-rounded.

The reason work and life seem to be in direct conflict so often is simple. The time and energy required for each comes out of the same pie. Each must take from the other, because the pie is finite. Here is what the conflict can often feel like.

Remember the 800-pound gorilla?

Imagine that you share your house, your personal living space, with an 800-pound, silverback lowland gorilla. This is a very large, strong, aggressive wild animal. When you come home, he is at the door. He has been in the house alone all day. As you squeeze through the front door, imagine how much of your house you would have to yourself. This is a wild gorilla, mind you. How much space would he leave you *in your own house*?

You would be relegated to the very edges of the rooms. The gorilla would take everything else for himself. Not only that, he would make a mess wherever he wants. Remember, this gorilla is not house trained at all.

Here's the metaphor. The gorilla is your nursing career. The house is your life.

What happens to your house when you live with a gorilla is a lot like what happens to your life when you choose nursing as a career. Your life outside of nursing often gets crowded out. You are left with only scraps along the edges for all your free time and important relationships. The career that was supposed to enable an extraordinary life can now dominate your life, leaving little room for anything else. Your career is also capable of stepping in at the most inopportune moments to make a mess of your life plans.

Gorilla taming

All is not lost. Gorillas can be house-trained, tamed, and shown healthy boundaries. You can lock him in the back bedroom so you and your family can have the rest of the house to yourselves. You can do the same with your nursing career when you know how. It will take a strategy to manage this balancing act. The following tools from Quadrant II of the Matrix are a good place to begin.

And let's get a couple of things crystal clear before we start.

- Whose gorilla is this?
- Who else has to live with this gorilla?
- So … whose responsibility is it to put some healthy boundaries around this beast?

THE SCHEDULE HACK

ONE OF THE laws of your work-life balance strategy is "the strongest structure wins." When we are talking about work life balance, structure is your calendar.

Let me ask you a quick question: do you carry a calendar with you most of the time?

I know your answer is yes. It is probably in your cell phone and you are never without your cell phone.

If I asked you to hand me your calendar, what would I find on it? It would have your work and call schedule for sure. After all, it is the calendar you carry to work.

What else is on this calendar?

Would I find any of the following?

- Your spouse or significant other's schedule?
- Your children's schedule?
- Your workout schedule?
- Your next date night?
- A manicure/pedicure, massage, yoga class?
- Your next vacation?
- Some blocked off free time for yourself to be with friends, take a walk, hike, bike ride, yoga or cooking class, or read a book for pleasure (heavens, just imagine that for a moment, will you)?

If you have all of those on the calendar you carry most of the time, congratulations. Take a moment to pat yourself on the back, because I have never seen it happen—and I have asked thousands of nurses what is on their calendars.

Understand this as an actual law of life balance.

Anything *not* on the calendar you are carrying is *not* going to happen, period.

One of the keys to taming the gorilla is to always carry something more than your work schedule with you. If you want to have time for your life, you must carry your Life Calendar with you at all times as well. Let me say that again.

If you want to have a life, *always carry your Life Calendar with you.*

The Schedule Hack is a simple process that takes only twenty minutes a week and ensures you always have your Life Calendar in your pocket or purse—without having to master any new technology. This is the first step in showing that gorilla some healthy boundaries.

The Schedule Hack has an added bonus as well. It will also bring you closer with your friends and family when they see you making them a priority every week.

Schedule Hack materials

1. The paper calendar you have hanging at home on the side of the fridge. It's the one with kitties or landscapes or your favorite poems you bought at Christmas. This calendar usually contains only the children's schedule or nothing at all.If you don't have a paper calendar on the fridge, I strongly suggest you buy one. They are not expensive and are the perfect tool for the Schedule Hack. NOTE: If you prefer to use an electronic calendar such as Google Calendar and are skilled with it, go for it. This version of the Schedule Hack is meant to be old-school so anyone can implement it today. If you and your family are facile with multiple Google Calendars at once, be my guest, as long as it actually works to create the work-life balance you seek. If it does not, I highly recommend this calendar-on-the-fridge method.
2. Some colored pens—your favorite kind.
3. Your cell phone.

SCHEDULE HACK PROCEDURE

Step One: Build Your Life Calendar for the Week Ahead

Pick a time in the week where everyone in your family or household is available. It could be just you or it could be you, your spouse or significant other, all your kids, and your parents who live over the garage. Whatever "family" is to you, pick a time when all of you can get together for twenty minutes or so. Sunday in late mornings often works well.

Pull that paper calendar off the fridge, grab the pens, and put them all on the kitchen table. Have everyone grab their calendars for the week ahead and put them on the table too.

Have some fun, be creative, and build your *life* calendar for the week ahead. Put everyone's schedule on it, using the colors however they make sense.

Remember, this is your LIFE Schedule

I know you will want to put your work schedule and call days on here automatically. Don't do it. You are already carrying your work schedule. This calendar is for your life outside of work. This is where you build your strategy to create more balance between your work and your larger life. This is where gorilla training begins.

Here comes the juicy part:

What do you want *for yourself* in the upcoming week? Remember, if you don't put it on your Life Calendar right here and now, it will not happen in the week ahead.

- Workouts
- Free time
- Coffee with an old friend or a relative
- Time to read a book for pleasure
- A class or hike
- A date night
- Manicure, pedicure, hot yoga, massage

Whatever you want, you must put it down on the calendar. Do it now (see the Weekly Bucket List training later in this section for more ideas).

Mandatory final scheduling action:

The last thing you put on the calendar is the date and time of your next Schedule Hack session. Everyone needs to be clear on when you will meet again. If I meet you on the street from now on and ask you to show me your Life Calendar, it must have your next Schedule Hack session on it—agreed?

Step Two: Take a Picture of Your Life Calendar with Your Cell Phone

Yes, it really can be that easy. Your Life Calendar for the week ahead can now be in your pocket at all times, available at the touch of a button right there on your cell phone.

When you are done, you will have a complete Life Calendar for the week ahead, written in colored pens, and captured in a picture on your cell phone. This week you will be a couple taps on your phone from being able to see your whole life and your complete circle of priorities.

Step Three: Defend Your Life Calendar

Now you are prepared to say the two-letter magic word of work-life balance. "No."

If someone at work asks you to take an extra shift or work a few extra hours, you can say, "Hang on a second, and let me check my calendar."

Open up your cell phone to the picture of your Life Calendar and see if you have a scheduled activity. If you are already booked, you can say, "I'm sorry, I have another commitment at that time. I won't be able to help out."

As you read the conversation above, does it make you a little uncomfortable? Most nurses squirm when I demonstrate this bit of dialogue. We are horrible at saying "no." Our discomfort has several sources.

- We are completely out of practice at saying "no." That is okay. Saying "no" is a skill you can practice. Remember, "Practice Makes _____."
- You don't want to be perceived as not being a team player. This is a variation on the prime directive of *never show weakness*.
- You may have a wave of guilt crash over you whenever you contemplate doing something for yourself—rather than for someone else.

Here is how to address these concerns.

a.) Practice

Stand in front of a mirror and practice several different ways to say "no" until you find a turn of phrase you are at least moderately comfortable with. Here are some examples:

- *I'm sorry, I have a previous engagement.*
- *Nope, I'm booked at that time.*
- *Looks like that time is taken, sorry.*
- *Not happening; looks like it's my date night* (if that is true).

The possibilities are endless. The key is to be prepared, practiced, and polished when the opportunity arises.

> ## Power Tip:
> **Role-play with your spouse or significant other. Have them be one of your partners—perhaps the one most likely to ask you to cover for them. You be yourself saying, "No."**
> **Rehearse until your spouse or significant other gives you at least a B+ for your performance. Have some fun here.**

b.) Release the Head Trash of "Always"

You will not always say "no" to this request when it comes at you. You can let "always" go. Let's shoot for 85 percent of the time, instead. The main reasons you won't say "no" are as follows:

- You owe this person. They covered for you at an earlier date and you want to settle the debt.
- You want this person to owe you down the road, so you can call on that debt in the future.
- You are not confident enough in your ability to say "no" yet to give it a shot. Time for more practice.

Here is how your Life Calendar will drive your behavior.

If you do say "yes" to someone's request—for whatever reason—you will immediately see who you have to get ahold of, apologize to, and reschedule with because you just threw your plans under the bus.

The Schedule Hack allows you to live your life in alignment with your complete circle of priorities.

And this is another tool that works every time you use it. The key is to put it into action now that you understand the principles involved.

Here is a common scenario. You certainly carry your work calendar at all times; I know that about you. If you are a parent, your kids' schedules are in that calendar too. Most likely, the only thing missing is you. If that is the case, a Schedule Hack upgrade is what you are looking for.

Keep doing your weekly calendar coordination with your family; just add yourself into the picture. Put your exercise schedule in there, your date nights, or some un-scheduled downtime.

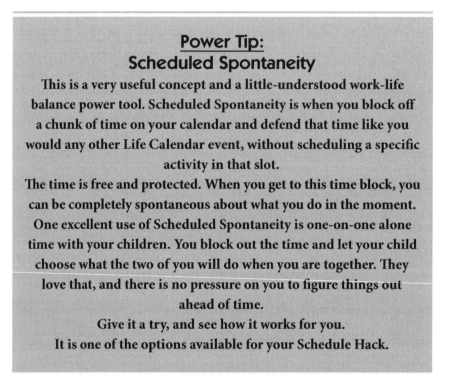

Power Tip:
Scheduled Spontaneity

This is a very useful concept and a little-understood work-life balance power tool. Scheduled Spontaneity is when you block off a chunk of time on your calendar and defend that time like you would any other Life Calendar event, without scheduling a specific activity in that slot.

The time is free and protected. When you get to this time block, you can be completely spontaneous about what you do in the moment. One excellent use of Scheduled Spontaneity is one-on-one alone time with your children. You block out the time and let your child choose what the two of you will do when you are together. They love that, and there is no pressure on you to figure things out ahead of time.

Give it a try, and see how it works for you.
It is one of the options available for your Schedule Hack.

Schedule Hack ACTION STEPS

- Who are the people on your Life Calendar?
- When is a good time for you all to do the Schedule Hack together?
- If you need to buy a paper calendar or pens, when will you do that?
- When will you do your first Schedule Hack? How can you make it fun?
- What things will you put on the calendar just for you?
- When will you practice saying "no?" (I dare you to practice with your spouse or significant other and find a way to make it fun!)
- Journal on your experience.

DATE NIGHT SECRETS

A STANDING ITEM on your Life Calendar *must* be a minimum of two date nights a month with your spouse or significant other.

Do not skip date night. Don't let it slide or forget to schedule it—even if you are single.

NOTE: If you do not have a significant other, date night could be an actual date with another person, time with a friend, or doing something nice or unexpected *all by yourself.* Yes, indeed, you can take yourself out on date night too.

Fun and adventure

When you are really busy, figuring out what to do on your date night can seem like just another item on your task list. I encourage you to do an attitude check here. What is more important to you—the 800-pound gorilla or some love, romance, adventure, and fun? Date night is a chance to break out of survival mode and do something extraordinary.

A few ideas

- Take turns deciding what you will do on date night. The one who is planning the date can't tell the other where you are going or what you are doing (other than what to wear).
- Each of you put three date night ideas on slips of paper and drop them into a hat. Pick one, raffle style, and go for it.
- Make it a game and set rules. Here is a fun one: Your date night can't involve calories or money.

Mandatory first date night action:

If you want to keep Date Night as a piece of your life balance strategy, I strongly encourage you to make this your first Date Night activity: before you order drinks or appetizers, schedule your next Date Night. Do it first thing on each date or you will quickly see your best intentions for a twice-a-month Date Night fizzle out. In the future, if I meet you in the street and ask you to show me your Life Calendar, it must have your next date night on it, agreed? (and your next Schedule Hack session … yes?)

Power Tip:

I encourage you to go the extra yard for date night. My challenge to you is to schedule a minimum of two date nights on your Life Calendar each month for the next three months—if your work schedule allows you to look that far into the future. That is a total of six date nights. Just walk over to the calendar on the fridge and write them in now.

Then your first action on your next date night is to add your sixth date night back onto the calendar three months from now. So if I stop you on the street you can always show me six date nights on your calendar at any given time. There's some work-life balance for you.

Date Night ACTION STEPS

- When is your next date night?
- Who is doing the planning?
- Discuss scheduling date nights out three months.
- Then, do it.
- Remember, your date night is not over until you have scheduled the next one and put it on both of your life calendars.
- Journal on your experience.

BUCKET LIST SECRETS

Bucket List (noun): *The list of things you want to do before you "kick the bucket."*

My clients and I find it very useful to build two bucket lists and use them as additional work-life balance tools.

1) Your BIG Bucket List

These are the classic *things I must do before I die*. The challenge with creating a meaningful BIG Bucket List is that most people put way too many things on it. This is why most people simply use their BIG Bucket List as a weapon to beat themselves up. If you put too many items on there, you will notice you never cross any of them off and feel supremely guilty. If this goes on for long enough, you may even give up on a bucket list as a useful way of looking at the world.

A real BIG Bucket List is not simply a list of things you want to check off before your time is up. An authentic BIG Bucket List contains the *life-altering, mind-bending things*, the ones that would break your heart if you were *not* able to accomplish them in this lifetime.

No one gets out of here alive. Now is the time to build that list and get on it, especially if the last couple of years or decades have been devoted to your career rather than your larger life. There is some rebalancing to be had.

Construct your BIG Bucket List

Write it all down. Keep it in the folder with your Ideal Career Description and Master Plan.

Test your BIG Bucket List

Put each and every item on your BIG Bucket List to this question, "If I got to the end of my life and had to acknowledge I had *not* completed this Bucket List item, how would that feel?"

If you are not heartbroken, torn up, mortified, and extremely sad and disappointed at the thought of never accomplishing this list item … *cross it off the list*.

It doesn't belong on this list unless it really hurts to imagine it left undone. Circle the ones that pass the test—the ones that would break your heart if you did not accomplish them. Those are your authentic BIG Bucket List items.

BIG Bucket List check off

Now, it is time to get one of these BIG bucket list items on your Life Calendar. Prioritize your list and pick just one. Plate spinning operates here as well. Once you have one BIG Bucket List item selected, there are only two steps to making it happen.

a) Put it on your schedule

Normally, these are pretty big-ticket items. They are not usually things you will do next week. Don't let this stop you from scheduling this important event.

The key is to look out on your calendar as far as you need to look. In some cases, it could even be next year or several years into the future. Look out until you can see the space you require to do this thing well, and block it off on a calendar you keep hanging on the wall in plain sight in your home or work space. You may have to buy or print off a calendar from three years in the future. That is fine. Find or print the calendar, block the time off, and hang it up where you can see it weekly.

b) Pay for the tickets.

If there is one thing that will get a nurse to actually take a trip, it is having skin in the game … by that I mean putting some money down. Once you have blocked off the time, step two is buy the tickets. Do it now. Whether it is Machu Picchu, the running of the bulls in Pamplona, visiting the country of your family's origin, a Spanish immersion school in Costa Rica, an Italian cooking class in Florence, rafting the Grand Canyon … get it scheduled and paid for, and it is highly likely to actually take place.

Afterward, it will take its rightful place in your memories as a peak experience, rather than a heartbreaking regret.

2) Your weekly Bucket List

What is your *one thing?*

Is there something you have found that is guaranteed to make your week special? You know, that one thing that whenever you manage to squeeze it in, it makes the whole week easier and sweeter? You say to yourself, "Man, I wish I could do that every week. It would make a huge difference for me."

Typically, these are activities you only manage to squeeze in every once in a while. I think you know what I am talking about. What is that activity that makes all the difference for you? This very short list is something I call your Weekly Bucket List.

Here are some examples I have heard from nurse clients:

- Cycling
- Running

- Yoga
- Hiking
- Coffee with a friend or colleague
- Alone time with each of your children—one-on-one
- Family play time as a whole family
- Reading a book for pleasure
- Meditation
- Mani-pedi
- Massage
- Date night (Yes, things can show up on multiple lists. It just shows how important they are.)
- Scheduled Spontaneity (see above)

Make your list. Write them down. Keep this list in the folder with your

- Ideal Career Description
- Master Plan
- BIG Bucket list

Make sure you bring your Weekly Bucket List items to your Schedule Hack each week. Putting these items on your Life Calendar is part of carving out time and space for you in your busy week. Defend these items just as vigorously as you do your work schedule to show that gorilla some healthy boundaries. I encourage you to drive them into your schedule with the Schedule Hack at an absolute minimum of twice a month.

More head trash - guilt can come up here

Some people have problems with guilt as they contemplate this concept of doing something just for themselves. A little voice saying, *What makes you think you are so special?* can pop up when you are blocking off time for your own personal use. This is your programming, pure and simple.

You can tell that voice, *Thank you for sharing* and do it anyhow. It is only when you are able to experience the pleasant things in your life that you can understand the difference that can make for you, your patients, your team, and your family.

Remember, plate spinning applies here as well. If yoga makes a night and day difference in your week, for example …

- Schedule one yoga class in the week ahead.
- Defend the schedule.
- Do it.
- See how it feels and whether you want to make yoga a Weekly Bucket List item in your Life Calendar going forward.

Bucket List secrets ACTION STEPS

- What's on your BIG Bucket List?
- Which items pass the test?
- Which BIG Bucket List item will you schedule and pay for first? When?
- What's on your Weekly Bucket List?
- Which one of your Weekly Bucket List items will you Hack into your schedule first?
- How can you make it an every week, or every other week, standing item?
- Journal on your experience.

THE BOUNDARY RITUAL

ONE OF THE keys to being able to recharge when you are not at work is creating a clean, solid, functioning boundary between work and home.

Leave work at work and come all the way home

There is an energetic boundary between work and home. In a normal situation, this would be like punching the time clock, changing your work clothes, and letting your roles and responsibilities fall away rather than dragging the stress, to-do lists, and the worries about patients home with you. Without a clean boundary between work and home, your energy and awareness remains at least partially focused on your career, even when you are not at work.

Without this clean boundary, rather than finding an oasis of rejuvenation at home, the drain of work stress continues.

Creating a Boundary Ritual is a skill you can learn and practice. It is the energetic equivalent of hanging up your role as a nurse like you would a white coat with your name embroidered over the breast pocket and checking out of your role as nurse. Your Boundary Ritual marks the boundary between work and home.

Your Boundary Ritual marks the transition from the environment where the patient comes first to one where *you* come first.

Fortunately, we have an excellent role model of a Boundary Ritual—Mr. Rogers.

Yes, *that* Mr. Rogers from *Mister Rogers' Neighborhood*, the children's television show on PBS.

You don't know what Mr. Rogers does before he walks through that door. It only takes a couple of shows to realize he is not the real Mr. Rogers until he has done three things. Remember them?

1. Put on his zip-up cardigan
2. Change his shoes
3. Sing his song, "It's a beautiful day in the neighborhood, a beautiful day for a neighbor—would you be mine? …"

With his Boundary Ritual complete, he is the slightly creepy Mr. Rogers we know and love for the rest of the show.

I have heard of nurses who naturally understand the importance of a Boundary Ritual. One night-shift nurse—a woman I worked with during my time in psych—shared with me how she used the tunnel she drove under as a "magic shield." When she entered the tunnel on the way out of work, it was as if she was washed clean of her career and entering into the "no work" zone. Each day as she drove home from work, she'd put on classical music, enter the tunnel, and remove her career-focus until another new workday.

I strongly encourage you to develop your own Boundary Ritual. It can be any action you wish, as long as your intention is to let go of being a nurse and come all the way home.

You have an excellent tool already available in the Squeegee Breath.

You also have a whole new set of Super Habit triggers within whatever routine it takes for you to get from your career to your home.

The simplest Boundary Ritual is to use a Squeegee Breath to release your role as nurse, using something you always do on your way home as your trigger. It could be exiting the hospital building as you walk out, taking the key out of your car's ignition at home, opening the door of your house, and many more.

Other actions you can use as Boundary Rituals include:

- Taking a shower
- Changing your clothes
- Taking out your contacts
- Going for a walk, run, or bike ride
- Walking the dog

What you use for a Boundary Ritual is not as important as having one in the first place. Set your intention to come all the way home. Feel the release of your nurse responsibilities as you perform your ritual and let the recharge soak in.

Don't be afraid to experiment here. Try different rituals out to see how they work. Remember Practice Makes _____ applies to your Boundary Ritual skills too. Switch things up and develop a small handful of your favorites. Smile, breathe, and release the nurse completely until the next time you need to put on your scrubs.

NOTE: There will be times when you are at home and still working, like when you are on call or have committee work you intend to do from home. I would not advise you to use the Boundary Ritual on those days simply because you are still in work mode and your nurse role. Save the Boundary Ritual for when you are actually off work —then, do the deed and form the boundary.

Power Tip:
A commute is an excellent place to build your Boundary Ritual. Pick some soothing music, put some items you find comforting on the dash of your car, take some deep breaths, and use the ride home as a decompression and extended release of your role as a nurse.

You can pack dozens of Squeegee Breaths into your drive and hit the front door with the nurse completely turned off.

Boundary Ritual ACTION STEPS

- What is your Boundary Ritual?
- When will you start using it?
- Journal on your experience.

QUADRANT III: ORGANIZATIONAL STRESS RELIEF

"Management is doing things right;
Leadership is doing the right things."
—Peter Drucker
"God grant me the serenity to accept the things I cannot change,
the courage to change the things I can,
and the wisdom to know the difference."
—The Serenity Prayer

QUADRANT III IS where you and your organization can work together to help lower your stress and prevent burnout. You can focus your cooperative efforts on creating a more nurse-friendly workplace—by design and on purpose.

The tools to create a more nurse-friendly work environment are simple common sense, just like everything you have learned so far. It only takes three steps to produce rapid, significant change inside an organization. I call these steps the Nurse Engagement Formula.

First, the Quadruple Aim

Let me tell you a story about the recent history of the United States' healthcare system from a macroeconomic level.

Ever since researchers began comparing the healthcare systems in various first world countries with regards to cost and quality decades ago, they noticed an interesting trend. In the USA, we spend far and away the most on healthcare of any nation in the world, but we don't get anywhere near the highest levels of population health or the longest lives. We spend much more and get much less.

In the 1990s, an organization called the Institute for Healthcare Improvement developed a focus for improvement efforts in America they called the "Triple Aim". The triple aim is a leadership stance where the organization maintains a laser focus on three things at once:

1. Lower cost
2. Higher quality
3. Better patient experience

If you look at most healthcare organization mission statements — including the mission statement for your organization most likely — you will see the Triple Aim in the words on the page.

We have over two decades' experience with the Triple Aim as a philosophy for improving a healthcare system. It has had unintended consequences. I think you will see quickly what is missing in the three sections of the Triple Aim. Do you see the gap?

What about the people providing the care?

Yes, the people are completely absent from the three priorities of the Triple Aim. The health and well-being of the people who deliver the care are completely left out of the equation.

The relentless focus on cost, quality, and patient experience, to the exclusion of every other success factor, has made a strong contribution to the burnout epidemic we are seeing today. Even the Institute for Healthcare Improvement no longer promotes the Triple Aim goals all by themselves.

Enter the fourth aim

In 2015, an article in *The Annals of Family Medicine*[13] titled, "From Triple to Quadruple Aim: Care of the Patient Requires Care of the Provider," proposes a fourth aim … the health and well-being of the providers of care.

With the new Quadruple Aim, it is imperative that any delivery system support all four components at once. Any initiative that delivers on only three of the four is not an optimal strategy.

Examples:

An initiative that produces better quality, lower cost, a better provider/staff experience, but creates a negative patient experience … is not optimal

And, for our discussion, any initiative that produces better quality, lower cost, a better patient experience, but heaps stress and additional work on the providers/staff … is not optimal. Sound familiar?

Adoption of the Quadruple Aim as a new level of awareness on the part of your organization's leadership team is an opportunity to restore balance to the patient care equation.

Unfortunately, word of the Quadruple Aim is spreading slowly through the leadership teams of healthcare organizations in the USA and the larger world. You may find yourself in an organization with a classic Triple Aim mission statement and a leadership team that has never heard of the concept. If you are in that situation, you have an opportunity to teach your leaders about the importance of the well-being of the nurses, doctors, and other staff.

Let me show you a framework for implementing the Quadruple Aim on your teams.

THE NURSE ENGAGEMENT FORMULA

1. Fill the educational hole around burnout.
2. Survey the nurses for their specific work stressors.
3. Address those concerns with a nurse-led Burnout Prevention Working Group.

When done well, these three steps will not only create a more nurse-friendly workplace, but they will also instill a culture of support, respect, and trust where one may have never existed before.

Let's take these steps one at a time.

1.) Fill the educational hole around burnout for physicians, nurses, and frontline staff

All burnout prevention efforts must start with education. I have already shown you how much of burnout's power lies in its ability to hide in our blind spots and programming. I have also shared a number of tools in Quadrants I and II that should be part of the normal education process of any nurse or doctor.

Unfortunately, we both know these concepts are not taught in nursing school or during orientation. In fact, the first time most nurses learn about burnout is when they are already in its downward spiral.

If you want to equip your nurses and staff with the tools to prevent burnout, the organization will have to take responsibility. You have taken responsibility for your own education by reading this book for personal benefit. Your organization can provide a training hub for all the providers and staff it employs.

You can pick a date to "out" burnout.

A comprehensive approach to this education process can even allow you to pick a date when everyone in your organization can recognize burnout and has Quadrant I and II tools to deal effectively with stress in the workplace.

I recommend a three-pronged approach:

a. Live burnout-prevention training such as our *Burnout Proof Live Workshop*.

b. Video burnout prevention training for those who cannot make the live event. Our *Burnout Prevention Resource Library* is an example.

c. Incorporate burnout prevention training into your onboarding process from now forward to maintain 100 percent awareness of burnout in the workplace.

Universal burnout education also produces some interesting cultural changes.

- It is no longer taboo to talk about stress, burnout, and work-life balance.
- It is no longer taboo to admit you are overstressed and reach out for help and support.
- Colleagues will begin to ask each other if they are okay, rising above the Lone Ranger, superhero, and *never show weakness* programming.
- Stress levels in the providers and staff begin to have a place in the leadership conversations throughout your organization.
- It sends a powerful message that the organization cares about its people—if steps two and three below follow in short order.

2.) Survey the nurses about their top three daily stresses

It is amazing to me how rarely organizations ask their nurses to name the top stresses in their workdays. If an organization does survey the nurses, it is usually with a huge, expensive third-party engagement survey of some sort. Typically, the results of the survey show burnout and disengagement without actually giving you any actionable information.

Ideally, you survey your nursing staff with a short, focused, inexpensive question set that gives you information you can put to use right away.

Here is my recommended question set:

- How would you rate your satisfaction with your career in our organization on a 1-10 scale?
- What is the #1 stressor in your workday?
- What is the #2 stressor in your workday?
- What is the #3 stressor in your workday?
- How would you describe the culture around here?
- What would you like the culture to be?
- Anything else?

I send these surveys out using Survey Monkey or Google Drive. They are fast and free. You will have your answers back in a matter of days. Notice that you can use the questions about the top stressors to create a weighted average and see immediately actionable data on what system flaws need to be addressed.

The nurses tell you exactly what is frying their bacon. They are pointing where they want the organization to pitch in. All you have to do is let them know you heard them and get on their concerns with meaningful action. That leads us to step three.

3.) Create a nurse Burnout Prevention Working Group to address the nurses' concerns

The best way for an organization to show it cares about the health of the providers in the front lines is to create, support, and fund a Burnout Prevention Working Group.

Note that this is not a committee. Committees have meetings. Most meetings in healthcare organizations are of stunningly poor quality.

A working group does work. The entire focus of this working group is to make progress in creating a more nurse-friendly workplace.

The project list for this group comes directly from the surveys outlined above. You asked the nurses a direct question. They have given you a direct answer. Now, it is time to take meaningful action.

It is critical that the working group receives funding and administrative support.

I see lots of burnout prevention committees with no staff and no budget. This guarantees it will fail to generate a meaningful and lasting response to the nurses' concerns. The meetings will dissolve into ineffective hand wringing.

Ideally, the Burnout Prevention Working Group is an arm of your existing nurse leadership structure. It must have nurses as its major participants. When this is true, the committee serves a dual purpose:

    a. It is a proactive force for positive change in the organization.

    b. The members of the group are able to hone their leadership and project management skills as they address the challenges identified by the survey. It is a training ground for your nurse leaders where they can practice leading successful projects. They are then able to bring their improved skills back into all facets of your nurse leadership activities.

The results

The three steps in the Nurse Engagement Formula—when they are done well—combine to continue producing positive changes in your group culture.

Your nursing staff will begin to notice and respond:

- "You taught me about burnout—how to recognize and prevent it."

- "You ask me what I would like changed around here and listen to what I have to say."
- "You are actually working to make my life better here at work."

These three steps build trust between the organization and the frontline staff. They start to shift from the Lone Ranger culture to one of mutual support and caring.

Unfortunately, less than 10 percent of organizations do anything like this, in my experience. It is a tremendous missed opportunity, especially here in the dawning of the Age of Engagement.

Instead, most organizations either are oblivious to or do not care about the health and well-being of their people.

Nothing says an organization does not care about its nursing staff more than when it fails to:

- Educate the nurses on burnout.
- Survey them on their major stressors.
- Work to proactively address their concerns.

Organizational Stress Relief ACTION STEPS

Work within your nursing leadership structure to persuade your organization to:

- Work with your organization to deliver burnout prevention training to all providers and staff.
- Survey your staff at least yearly with a set of questions that give you actionable information on lowering stress in the workplace.
- Create, fund, and support a Burnout Prevention Working Group.
- Use the survey results to identify a project that will have a stress-lowering impact.
- Lead the project, growing your nursing leaders on the way.
- Repeat the steps above.
- Journal on your experience.

For a complete overview of the Nurse Engagement Formula and to learn how you can get help building the three components within your organization, use this page to contact us directly:

www.StopNurseBurnout.com/contact

QUADRANT IV: ORGANIZATIONAL RECHARGE

"We are human beings, not human doings."
—Zen saying

"There is virtue in work and there is virtue in rest.
Use both and overlook neither."
—Alan Cohen

Normalize the expectation of work-life balance

AS PART OF the organizational commitment to health and wellness for the nursing staff, there is a parallel commitment and expectation that nurses will have a full life outside of their careers. This is the basis for the institutional support of part-time work and reasonable vacation allowances.

Being a nurse and simultaneously being a healthy human being must become pillars of the culture within your organization. This is the essence of the true Quadruple Aim.

Methods to improve the work-life balance include:

- On-site Programs
  - On-site exercise facilities and exercise classes
  - Walking groups at lunch
  - On-site massage and guided imagery library
  - On-site programs to teach healthcare stress management and burnout prevention
  - On-site programs to teach and allow the practice of mindfulness, meditation, and other stress relief tools (yoga, Tai Chi, etc.) to nurses and staff during workdays
- Organization-centered social activities, parties, charity events, and onsite clubs
- Organizational participation in community charity activities with nurses and staff invited to participate
  - When you participate, you are representing your organization to the larger community and connecting with staff and colleagues outside the workplace.
  - It can be a refreshing change from the office or hospital environment.

- ➤ You can connect in different ways with your colleagues, staff, their families, and your patients.
- ➤ It is a chance to bear witness to the larger good you are doing in your town.
- Off-site tours and excursions for the nurses and staff sponsored by the organization
- Establishing and supporting a "culture of caring"
  - ➤ Establish the expectation that nurses check in with your partners and colleagues about how they are doing
  - ➤ Help partners get support if it appears to be needed, without stigma
  - ➤ Share outside interests

NOTE: Success indicators for a "culture of caring" are "yes" answers in your surveys to the following questions from the book *First Break all the Rules* by Marcus Buckingham and Curt Coffman:

- Does someone at work seem to care about me as a person?
- Is there someone at work who encourages my development?
- In the last seven days, have I received praise or recognition for good work?

Organizational Recharge ACTION STEPS

Look at the list of Quadrant IV options above and pick one to explore, experiment with, or launch in your organization. All of these can be fun, creative, out-of-the-box experiences.

NOTE: You are probably being called to be a leader here as well. If these things are not happening in your organization right now, they are not likely to appear spontaneously anytime soon. These are recharge-enhancing ideas that require the breath of life from a willing and enthusiastic leader. If that is you, what plate will you spin up first?

Journal on your experience.

CHAPTER 5

NO ONE IS AN ISLAND

Leadership and Communication Skills for Nurses

"Coming together is a beginning.
Keeping together is progress.
Working together is success."
—Henry Ford

"None of us is as smart as all of us."
—Ken Blanchard

TEAM LEADERSHIP SKILLS FOR NURSES

As you begin to build your Ideal Career, you will quickly notice how damaging Lone Ranger programming can be. No one is an island. There is no way you can possibly reach your career goals without the help of your team. This is equally true at home.

Even if you decided to let go of the Lone Ranger and learn how to collaborate with your team more effectively, you are still at a disadvantage because of the leadership skills you learned in your training. Here is what you were taught to do:

- Figure out everything all by yourself
- Delegate tasks to non-licensed personnel
- Rarely accept help from anyone

That's not a very functional way to lead people, unless you really liked your drill sergeant in basic training.

Let me show you how this built-in leadership paradigm sets you up to work way too hard and never really get the best ideas out on the table before you take action. It is a recipe for struggle that is hidden in the way a nurse is taught to work with a team. You must expose and reprogram your leadership skills to share the work of building your Ideal Career with your team.

When this is done well, your team and family will be key allies in your success and happy to play their role from the start.

WHEN THE LONE RANGER WORKS ... AND WHEN IT DOESN'T

As we pass through the years of nursing school and clinical orientation, we gradually and inevitably inherit the central role of the clinical care team. We are seen as leaders because of our specialized skills and knowledge base. Our position at the center of the clinical care team is automatic once we begin to care for patients full time.

Along the way, you also inherit a leadership style that will radically compromise your ability to create your Ideal Career unless we expose it here and now.

We are never fully trained in leadership skills and often exhibit confused behaviors. This style is audible in the language we use to describe how a nurse relates to the team.

On one hand, the nurse "delegates tasks," and the team is expected to carry them out. We tell people what to do.

In the same shift, we receive orders from physicians and are expected to obey them. We are told what to do.

In the process, we are caught in the middle, doing and delegating as quickly as possible. We put all the responsibility on our own backs like good superhero Lone Rangers and fail to let the team design the team's work.

This unspoken and untrained leadership style has negative consequences for everyone involved:

- The nurse works too hard trying to coordinate everything and everybody by sheer personal effort.
- You feel like you have to do everything for your patient personally and asking for help is a sign of weakness.
- The support staff is turned into "sheep" waiting for the nurse to tell them what to do. They are waiting for delegated tasks and hesitate to act without a direct command.
- Much of the skills and experience of your team go to waste. You don't ask what they think, they don't volunteer their opinions without being asked, and poor decisions are made and acted on all the time.

This Lone Ranger style is inherent in the structure of the nursing team because we rarely receive education on how to be effective leaders in nursing school. In addition, many of our nursing leaders have not received any formal training themselves, so the role models we look up to are Lone Rangers too. So, we naturally and automatically fall back onto our programming to do everything ourselves—especially when we are under stress.

What about all the other activities that go into the day-to-day functioning of your patient care team and your larger organization—the basics of patient flow, administration, operations, and personnel issues? Your team (including your manager and the nurse leaders above you) will want to look to you as a leader, even in these non-clinical areas where, in reality, you feel like you have no control over the decision-making. The person delegating tasks (you) often lacks the confidence and training to step into leadership roles in the workplace.

Example:

How often does a member of your team bring up a question about operations? Something like, "Nurse Jane, what should we do about these infection reports? I know we track them month-to-month, but there's got to be a better way to manage this data."

How should you know? You spend your day on the floor with patients. You don't have time to follow the reports and don't have a clue about where to find them in the nursing data dashboards. You are simply not qualified to give an answer. If you do chime in, it will not be an informed opinion.

That won't stop the Lone Ranger in you from giving it a shot, though.

There you sit, the nurse who can handle it all. Everyone is waiting for an answer. You and your Lone Ranger programming make the mistake of giving one because after all, the buck stops here ... right? You are flying by the seat of your pants, hoping this turns out well.

You give an answer, a discussion ensues, you feel like you dodged a bullet, and at the same time, you know there must be a better way to be a leader. In the end, your idea is not the best and it takes three or four meetings and a couple of months to address the issue well.

This happens every day in nursing committees around the world. It does not have to be this way.

Reality check

To build your Ideal Career, you must engage your entire team. You must switch out the Lone Ranger for a true Team Captain. Your leadership must extend beyond your purely clinical activities and into non-clinical areas like patient flow and the flow of documentation.

You and your team must excel at all the activities that take place on the outside while you are in the room with the patient. This is different from delegating tasks.

Excellence in your entire career takes a different leadership skill set. No passive confusion or top-down Lone Ranger.

THE TEAM CAPTAIN

Let me show you a whole different collaborative nurse leadership style I call the "Team Captain." This leadership style is one where:

- You don't have to work so hard.
- You tap the skills and experiences of your whole team—together you come up with the answers because they are also experts in their roles.
- The whole team is engaged and enthusiastic from the start.

There are just three simple steps to help you let go of your Lone Ranger. Let me show you the steps and give you an example of what they look like in action.

Three steps to the team captain

1.) Set and Hold the Vision and Goal

This is one of Steven Covey's "seven habits of highly effective people." As he says, "Begin with the end in mind."

One of the Team Captain's most important skills is setting the Vision and giving the team an outcome Goal. In the example of the tracking infection reports above, the target could be:

Get the infection reports from the charts to the centralized nursing database two weeks before the committee meeting each month.

Setting the vision and goal frames the team discussion from this point forward. This goal keeps everyone on target, moving to your vision of success.

2.) Ask Powerful Questions

This is another skill set we didn't learn in nursing school or orientation. The ability to ask powerful, open-ended questions is key to the Team Captain nurse leadership style.

The simplest way to ensure your questions are always open-ended is to start them with either:

"What …"

Or

"How …"

A question beginning with *what* or *how* can't be answered with a yes or no. When faced with this kind of a question, the listener must think first and then answer with a complete thought. (These are fabulous questions for your patient assessments as well.)

These questions are the foundation for tapping into your team's skills and experience.

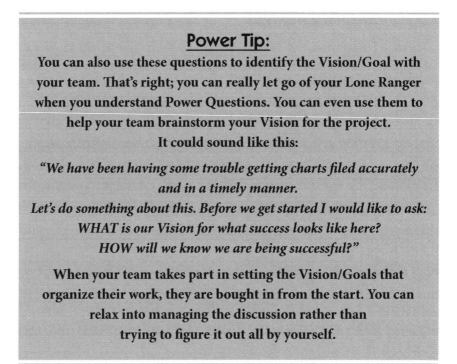

Power Tip:

You can also use these questions to identify the Vision/Goal with your team. That's right; you can really let go of your Lone Ranger when you understand Power Questions. You can even use them to help your team brainstorm your Vision for the project.
It could sound like this:

"We have been having some trouble getting charts filed accurately and in a timely manner.
Let's do something about this. Before we get started I would like to ask:
WHAT is our Vision for what success looks like here?
HOW will we know we are being successful?"

When your team takes part in setting the Vision/Goals that organize their work, they are bought in from the start. You can relax into managing the discussion rather than trying to figure it out all by yourself.

3.) Listen and Hold the Problem-Solving Context

As the Team Captain, you are responsible for creating and maintaining the *context* in which your *team* solves the *team's* problems. Your job is to create and maintain a team environment where people collaborate and cooperate, working together to solve the team's problems—rather than you simply telling them what to do.

To accomplish this as a nurse leader, you must …

- Hold the Vision
  - ➤ "Remember everyone, our Vision of success here is having infection reports flow from the clinical chart to the nursing database two weeks before our committee meetings happen."
- Ask Powerful Questions—Starting with "What" or "How"
  - ➤ "What are your thoughts on how we can make that happen?"
  - ➤ "How would you suggest we change the way we do things now?"
- Lead the discussion with questions, rather than giving orders. This maintains the environment of collaboration.
  - ➤ Be open to everyone's input.
  - ➤ Use the best ideas on the table, no matter where they came from.

Trusting your team and engaging them from the start is the essence of Team Captain leadership. Powerful Questions are the key tool that will make all the difference.

Remember, *you* don't have to come up with all the answers.

Figuring out all the answers and giving orders is the Lone Ranger. Go ahead and let him or her go. When you are that kind of nurse leader, you are working too hard and the team is never equipped with the best ideas.

With these new Team Captain leadership skills, you will begin to notice something very interesting. This realization flies in the face of everything you were taught about being a leader.

You don't need all the answers if you have:

- A Vision
- Powerful Questions
- A Team

> ## Power Tip:
> Now, you will have your own ideas on solutions. You and I both know that. Just remember, if this is not purely a nursing issue—if it has anything to do with patient flow or things that go on outside of the patient room—you may not be the most qualified person on the team.
>
> The Team Captain's goal is simple: get the best ideas out on the table by tapping the skills and experience of every single member of your team.
>
> You lead the discussion using your Powerful Questions.
>
> Save your ideas until last.
>
> Add your input only at the end, and see if it adds to the discussion. If your ideas work, and the team agrees, use them. If someone else has a better suggestion, use that idea. Whatever you do, don't just wade in and start telling people what to do or giving orders from the start. This will shut your team down and leave you with only a fraction of the value your team could bring with a more collaborative context.

Example #1

Team problem solving

Let's use the case of the infection data reports above. Here is what a Team Captain, a collaborative nurse leader, might do with this issue.

You discuss the problem with the infection control committee and agree the goal is to have the infection data all entered into the nursing dashboard within two weeks of the monthly meeting.

You pull the entire committee together (your monthly infection control meeting is ideal for this).

Lead the meeting off with something like this:

We have had some issues with getting infection data from the chart into our nursing database appropriately and in a timely fashion. Going forward, our goal as a team is to figure out a way to get all infection data from the charts to the dashboard within two weeks of our scheduled monthly meeting.

I am not the expert here and want us to design this system as a team.

We need everyone's input to build a system that works for all of us.

<u>Start asking powerful questions:</u>

- What are your thoughts on how we could get the infection data into the dashboard?
- How do you suggest we approach this issue?
- What are the things we are doing now that seem to work at least a little bit?
- How can we do more of these things?
- What things are not working?
- How can we change them to hit our goal?
- Which members of our team need to be involved in this new system?
- How can we make this so it involves as few people and as few touches of paper as possible?
- How can we make it so this infection data reporting system does not interfere with the activities of caring for our patients?
- How will we track the performance of this new system?
- What is our next step?
- Who is the manager of this project?
- When will we meet to discuss this again?

In a short period of time, your team will design this system. You don't have to have the answers. You have the Powerful Questions and focus them on the Vision/Goal of your ideal outcome.

Because the team was involved in designing the system from the start, they are fully bought in and engaged. They don't have to obey an order from you. They are carrying out an action plan they helped create. Creating this action plan tapped into the skills and experience of the whole team.

Goodbye, Lone Ranger.

Hello, Team Captain.

Example #2:

The effective monthly committee meeting

Ideally, your Team Captain skill set is on full display in your monthly infection control or other team meetings. I know from bitter experience just how much time poorly run meetings can waste. Typically, you have plenty of things to do back on the unit ... right?

Many teams have such negative experiences in meetings that they skip them all together. *Not* a good idea. A well-run meeting is the key to building a better team.

If you don't take time to step out of the flow of the way you do things now—as a complete team—and work on improving your current systems, things will never improve. You will be putting out one fire after another. You must work *on* your career, not just *in* your career, to make progress toward your Ideal Career Description. If utilized properly, monthly committee meetings like this are the best way to encourage your team to help you get there.

Try these steps:

- Have a basket where you and your team members can put suggestions, problems, and questions during the workday. The contents of this basket are the raw materials for your committee meeting.
- At the meeting, set aside time on each agenda to run through the items in the basket.
- Help your team prioritize and pick *one* (plate spinning) issue to work on.
- Ask Powerful Questions to generate a team Vision for the ideal outcome on this issue.
- Use Powerful Questions to gather the best ideas for action steps.
- Continue to use Powerful Questions to generate a realistic action plan.
- Kick your action plan into gear.
- Follow up on this project at your next meeting.

Power Tip:

Normally, the basket of topics for your monthly staff meeting will only contain items the team members see as a problem. You can expand your team's ability to make rapid positive changes by asking a couple more Power Questions:

- What is not working, and how can we fix it?
- What *is* working, and how can we do more of it?
- What can we stop doing?
- What can we start doing that we don't do now?
- What else?

Switching to Team Captain and Powerful Questions will dramatically improve your effectiveness as a leader—without working harder

These simple skills are always applicable, from your monthly staff meeting to the boardroom of a Fortune 100 corporation. In fact, these so called "soft skills" are the foundation of any effective leader's toolbox. They are typically not covered in formal leadership education such as an MBA program, even in this depth.

TEAM CAPTAIN LEADERSHIP SUMMARY

You don't need all the answers when you have:

- A Vision
- Powerful Questions
- A Team

As the Team Captain, you must:

- Hold the Vision.
  - › You can ask questions to generate the Vision too.
- Ask Powerful Questions starting with "what" or "how."
- Lead the discussion with questions, rather than giving orders.

Team Captain Leadership ACTION STEPS

- In what situations or roles do you feel the strongest urge to have all the answers and tell everyone what to do (give orders)?
- In what situations do you feel like you have to do it all by yourself, and you can't ask for help?
- In what situations do people look to you for orders and answers and you are uncomfortable giving an opinion because you know you are not the best qualified to answer?
- Write down some Powerful Questions that could help the team clarify their Vision of a successful outcome.
- Write down some Powerful Questions that could help the team build an action plan.
- Decide when and where you will try out at least one of your Powerful Questions.
- Journal on your experience.

HOW TO MANAGE YOUR BOSS

According to the Bureau of Labor Statistics' Employment Projections for 2012 to 2022 released in December of 2013, nursing is listed among the top occupations in terms of job growth through 2022. The RN workforce is expected to grow from 2.71 million in 2012 to 3.24 million in 2022, an increase of 526,800 or 19 percent. However, this projected growth is unlikely to bring with it any increase in professional autonomy.

Within the bureaucracy of a large healthcare organization, you are no longer in charge of your patient care. You are expected to follow organizational policy and meet specific patient care quotas. You also find yourself positioned firmly in the middle of a large organizational chart with layers of bosses above you. Your managers often have the frustrating ability to dictate the specifics of your career, unless you figure out a way to have some influence on their decisions.

Let me show you three keys to managing your boss if you are an employed nurse. These are the tools you need to make your boss an ally in creating your Ideal Career.

Have you ever asked yourself this question?

"If I am not the boss, how do I manage the person who is?"

As an employed nurse, you know your organizational leadership chart shows you the effective chain of command. You are most likely somewhere in the middle of that chart. You have a boss and you also have people who report to you and see you as their boss.

You just learned some Team Captain skills, so you know a thing or two about leading and managing your direct reports and team members. What about managing your boss?

I know they did not cover "boss management" in nursing school. And I want you to know this is not a situation where you simply keep your head down and learn how to deal with the frustrations of not being in charge more effectively. You must somehow manage this person if you are going to find any wiggle room to create your Ideal Career.

Like it or not, the quality of your relationship with your boss is a huge factor in your quality of life.

- A good relationship can provide you with a powerful advocate for your Ideal Career.

- A poor relationship with your immediate supervisor can lead to burnout and is one of the top three reasons nurses quit their jobs.

THREE KEYS TO MANAGING YOUR BOSS

1.) Understand Your Boss X2

It is vitally important to understand your boss on two key levels:

a.) Know his or her personality and communication style

Is your boss an action-oriented person who wants the bullet points before making a quick decision, or a detail-oriented, introverted "engineer type" who requires all the information and a good chunk of time to decide how to proceed? Or, someone completely different?

Study your boss and his or her communication style very carefully. Pretend you are an anthropologist, carefully observing your boss as a key member of your "tribe."

- How does he or she schedule his or her days?
- How does he or she prefer to be communicated with - email, text, phone, or in person?
- How do the people who have the best working relationships with your boss relate to this person? What success factors can you identify and emulate?

Then, practice the Platinum Rule: "Treat people how they want to be treated."

Match your boss's communication style and personality when the two of you are together. Give him the information and time he wants, just the way he wants it, especially when you are making a request for change to your work structure.

b.) Know your boss's goals and priorities

Your boss almost certainly has a boss. She has her own personal set of goals and orders from above.

Do you know what her priorities, goals, and objectives are? The easiest way to find this out is to ask her directly and take good notes. It will be much easier for you to get what you need from your boss if your request aligns with one of her own goals. This is the essence of a win-win solution.

- What are her key objectives for this quarter and this year?
- What role does she see you playing in reaching these goals?

2.) Understand Yourself X2

You must understand yourself on these same two levels.

a.) What is your personality and communication style and how does it differ from those of your boss?

Notice the way you naturally communicate and how that either matches or conflicts with your boss's personality and style. In most cases, you will need to modify the way you communicate to connect effectively with your boss.

Remember, you are striving for the Platinum Rule here. *Treat people the way they want to be treated.* So, if your boss likes all the details and time to consider his decision, give him just what he wants: details and time.

b.) What are your goals and needs?

If you have created your Ideal Career Description and are using your Master Plan to continuously improve your work, you will probably have requests for your boss every month.

Winning your boss's support will be the key to making some of the career changes you require. Your Master Plan helps you pinpoint exactly how you need your boss to contribute to your success.

- Do your best to align your needs with one of his goals, and create the win-win that pleases both of you.
- Then, ask for what you want.

You may need to negotiate back and forth and be willing to accept a bit of a compromise. Do not let that stop you from being clear on what you want and then asking for it.

3.) Manage Your Relationship

Let's face it—you can't actually manage your boss. You are not in the position in the org chart for that. What you can manage is the relationship between you. Most nurses miss this point altogether. Here's how that relationship usually works.

You may see your boss only a couple of times a year, and most often that is when she calls you into her office to tell you there is a problem.

That is actually the absence of a relationship.

You can't manage a vacuum. The chance of you getting something you need from your boss when this is the nature of your relationship is close to zero.

You must manage the relationship proactively. Think of it this way: your relationship is another example of an energetic bank account. This time the energy it holds is *trust*.

Every positive interaction makes a deposit of trust and goodwill into this account. You will need a balance of trust to draw on if there is a conflict or problem. If you only see your boss when she stops by to tell you about something that is not working, you have nothing to draw on. No matter what the exact conversation is about, it will drive the two of you even farther apart.

THE TRUST SOLUTION

Have regular collegial meetings with your boss to make sure you are on the same page. Make trust deposits in these meetings so your relationship has something to draw on when you need it.

How often should you meet? Once a month like clockwork is very helpful. Once a quarter is a bare minimum. Your objective is to get to know him and his goals and let him know your goals and challenges.

Here are some questions to ask:

- What are your goals for this quarter and this year?
- What role do you see me playing in those goals?
- How else can I help you get there?
- How do you evaluate my performance, and what are the most important numbers for you?
- How am I doing at this time?
- What do you see as ways I can improve?
- What is something you see on the horizon that I can start preparing for now?

Down the road, these are also the conversations where you can ask for what you need to keep creating your Ideal Career.

Keep working to make deposits in your relationship bank account with your boss. Shoot for a ratio of positive 5:1, meaning five positive interactions to every one negative or uncomfortable one. This way, your Trust Account with your boss will always be in positive territory.

Don't be a whiner!

The typical nurse will point to a problem and ask the boss, "What are you going to do about this?" Notice this is a classic phrase a victim uses. It is complaining, pure and simple. It is incredibly common, and it will destroy your relationship and make you adversaries immediately. You will blow any chance of your boss helping you create your Ideal Career if you communicate with him in this fashion.

This doesn't mean you can't ask your boss for help with the problems you are facing. However, if you change your communication just a little bit, you will bring your boss into a position of being your ally rather than your biggest frustration. Here is a rule to follow:

Any time you bring your boss a problem, **always** *bring a solution too.*

You are a problem solver. It only takes a little more effort to think of a solution or two before you go talk to your boss. You are also able to see the difference between a problem and a dilemma; your boss probably doesn't understand this distinction. You can teach him the difference. This allows you to shift from being just another whining nurse to the two of you working on an effective strategy as a team.

Ideally, your solution or strategy is a win-win that accomplishes two things at once:

1. It gives you more of what you want.
2. It meets one of your boss's objectives at the same time.

Remember the "Continuation Rule"

Every interaction you have with your boss (or any other person for that matter) sets the stage for your next encounter.

- If you end on a positive note, your next meeting will continue on that same positive trajectory—even if your discussion is about a problem.
- If the meeting ends badly, you will start the next one in the pits as well.
- Do everything you can to avoid ending any meeting in a negative fashion.

Managing your boss ACTION STEPS

1.) Begin to observe your boss closely and take notes.

Prepare yourself to begin practicing the Platinum Rule. Know how your boss communicates and makes decisions.

Arrange a meeting in the absence of any problems or crisis. Call up your boss and tell her something like this:

- *I would like to buy you a cup of coffee and get to know your goals for me—and the larger organization—so we are always on the same page.*
- *I would like to be a better team player.*
- *I know you are a very important member of the team here, and I would like to see how we can each do a better job of supporting each other.*
- *When can we get together?*

Let her determine the place and time; then, get to work on your specific question list for the conversation.

2.) Create your list of questions.

3.) Hold the meeting, keep it real, and take great notes.

- Make sure that your conversation adds to your relationship Trust Account while being real about your concerns. This may be your first collegial interaction, so do not ask for any changes just yet.
- Set yourself a goal to increase your knowledge base about your boss's personality, leadership, decision-making style, and goals and objectives.
- Get to know your boss as a person too. Does he have children, outside interests, or hobbies? Where do the two of you have common ground?
- Take great notes, just like you would with a patient. Always add to your knowledge base and building your relationship.

4.) Schedule your next meeting.

Make a habit of scheduling your next visit with your boss before this one is done, so you always have a relationship-building meeting on the books with him before you walk out the door. Quarterly is great. Monthly or every other month is better. Ideally, you should put the whole year's worth of meetings on your calendars at once before this first one is over.

5.) Keep your ideal career description and master plan up to date.

Know the latest version of your Ideal Career Description and Master Plan. Keep track on the action steps that require your boss's assistance and support.

6.) Build a win-win, and ask for it.

Pick the highest priority change you want to make to your career. Look at it from two perspectives: yours *and* your boss's. Put yourself in your boss's shoes now that you know more about him and his situation.

Do your best to create a solution that will be a *win* for *both* of you. Prepare to present this request at your next meeting.

7.) Rehearse your conversation.

Never, ever go into these conversations cold. Brainstorm your boss's most likely questions and objections, and prepare responses to them. Practice your responses in the mirror so you are prepared when you are face-to-face.

> ## Power Tip:
> **Use your team here. Significant others can be the perfect people to play your boss in your rehearsals. They have heard your stories and often surprise nurses by giving an Oscar-worthy performance. They usually participate with gusto when invited to help you prepare for this conversation.**

8.) Be flexible and willing to negotiate.

Make sure you have a positive balance in your relationship Trust Account before you make any requests and that your last encounter with your boss was a positive one. Use the Squeegee Breath before and during your conversation to keep your cool. Engage in as much give and take as necessary to ensure your boss is aware of your flexibility.

9.) Be patient.

Leaders and administrators do not have the same finely-tuned sense of urgency as a clinician. You may not reach a happy agreement in this first meeting. Don't accept an outright *no* at this point. Keep this as an ongoing discussion for future meetings. If you re-address this issue over time, you are likely to find new ideas that make it possible down the road. Do not give up if this is important to you. Apply your creativity, and stay in a relationship with your boss.

The result

When my coaching clients apply these boss management skills, they are often surprised at the flexibility, support, and positive working relationship that results. In many cases, things you thought were impossible—like going to part-time or getting additional support staff for your unit—are immediately available when you first put yourself in your boss's shoes and then present a win-win request to her.

THE LEADERSHIP MASTER SKILL

How to say "Thank You" with impact

As you recover from burnout or move in the direction of your Ideal Career, you will soon realize that your success hinges in large part on how you engage with and manage your teams. "No one is an island," and no nurse is one, either. You must have a team in the workplace and another one at home to be successful. It helps when they enjoy the experience of being on your team too.

You have learned the Team Captain leadership paradigm. Now, let me show you what I consider to be the Master Skill of a quality Team Captain—how to say "thank you" with impact.

Effort vs. Skill

Research coming from parenting experts gives us a window into the most effective way to say thank you.[14] The two common patterns of thanks are to acknowledge a person's skill or a person's hard work. Here's how the two of them sound:

- "You are very good at that. Thanks a lot. I really appreciate it."
- "Thanks for your hard work. I really appreciate it."

Which one do you think is more effective? It is the acknowledgment of *effort*. If you are good at anything, it is because you have put in the hard work to hone your skills. When you say thanks, I encourage you to acknowledge effort.

Practice until you are comfortable

Many nurses say "thank you" in a rush, if at all. It's that darn blind spot that keeps us focused on problems, errors, and the gap. Most of us are relatively awkward at thanking others or simply overlook it. So, let me give you some tips.

Short and Sweet

Pick a phrase that works for you, one that is short and to the point. For example, "Thanks for your hard work. I/the patient/the team really appreciate it." Then, practice it in the mirror until you are comfortable and it feels natural to you.

Catch Them Doing Something Right

Look for opportunities to catch your colleagues doing a good job. Thank them right on the spot. Don't be afraid to acknowledge them in a public setting within earshot of others.

- Square your posture to face them directly.
- Look them in the eye.
- Thank them and …
- Move on.

Well done.

Bonus:

Just so you know, you probably just delivered a triple whammy deposit into their Energy Accounts with this one simple act (see Chapter 1).

How often should you thank your people?

Simple: whenever you see a reason to. Research shows that once a week is about right.[15] Now, I don't advise you make a checklist and thank everyone once a week whether they deserve it or not. That would take all the meaning and authenticity out of your gratitude. Be on the lookout for reasons to thank your people for their hard work, and you will see them every day. Then, don't hold back on saying thank you. We all know that without these people, you would never get home.

THANK YOU SUMMARY

- Practice saying thank you until you are comfortable.
- Acknowledge effort and all progress.
- Catch your colleagues doing something right.

Thank you ACTION STEPS

- Choose your thank-you phrase(s).
- Practice them until you are comfortable.

- Be on the lookout for opportunities to thank your people for their effort and your team's progress toward your Ideal Career.
- Whom do you owe a thank-you to right now?
- When will you thank them?
- Repeat the last two questions, thinking about your "home team" and family.
- Journal about your experience.

CHAPTER 6

DO I HAVE TO CHANGE JOBS?

When to Leave and How to Find Your Ideal Job This Time Around

"There are risks and costs to action.
But they are far less than the long-range risks of comfortable inaction."
—John F. Kennedy

"Great minds have purposes, others have wishes."
—Washington Irving

I am frequently asked how often an actual job change is necessary to recover from burnout. Here is my experience.

If I meet a nurse before they have made the decision to quit, about 70 percent end up recovering from burnout without having to change jobs. They use their Ideal Career Description and their Master Plan to reach enough overlap in their Venn of Happiness that they don't feel a need to move on. These three concepts create a framework for moving your current job more in alignment with your ideal job that is completely adjustable to any nurse's specific situation.

The process of recovery takes approximately three to nine months, and each nurse ends up building a burnout prevention strategy containing three to five components. When you have your Master Plan in that folder, the process for increasing the overlap of your Venn of Happiness is straightforward. You have the blueprint right in front of you. All you have to do is take the action steps required.

Whether or not you will need to change jobs depends upon your success implementing your Master Plan and the fundamental characteristics of your current workplace and your current boss. If you can't get the overlap between this job and your Ideal Job up to a percentage you are comfortable with—for most nurses this is anything 60 percent or greater—changing job positions may be the answer.

For example, you may reach a point where you have used the tools in this book to make some changes over the course of several months. Let's say you notice your Venn of Happiness overlap increases from a baseline of 40 percent to its current position of 55 percent, and the improvement has stalled there. You consult your Ideal Career

Description and the remaining steps on your Master Plan and conclude this is as good as it is going to get in your current position.

My question to you will be a simple one. Is 55 percent good enough to stay in this position? You get to decide. However, I want to make sure you avoid the major mistakes I see many nurses making when they look for a new job. Without the tools below, it is not uncommon to find changing jobs to be the very definition of jumping out of the frying pan and into the fire.

TWO NURSE JOB SEARCH MISTAKES YOU MUST AVOID

DANGER: I have consulted with numerous nurses who stepped right into these two job search traps. They usually contact me after changing jobs when the new job turns out to be even worse (often much worse) than the one they left behind. Don't let this happen to you.

1.) Do not quit *this* job.

I encourage you to stay put, keep your head down, use the Quadrant I stress relief tools in Chapter 4, and stay in your current position while you look for your new job, if at all possible. I know you might be in an emergency situation where you must get out, but anything short of an emergency, I encourage you to stay and build a solid transition plan.

Realize that once you make the decision to leave, this job is now your bridge to a better future. If you quit without a plan, you will probably put yourself under a lot of financial pressure and may damage your resume. Unless you must leave now, stay put and let's build you a transition plan to a more Ideal Career.

This advice is even more important if you are in a position of financial weakness. If you are in debt with a negative net worth and do not have at least enough savings for six months of your bills, staying put is imperative. Your financial situation will drive you to make decisions out of desperation, and you and everyone in your family are highly likely to suffer needlessly.

If you implement the Squeegee Breath, the Schedule Hack, and the Boundary Ritual—adding in the BID Huddle and some team building (all in Chapter 4)—most nurses will be able to stop the downward spiral in their energy while they conduct a high quality job search.

This job is your bridge to a better place.

This job can provide for you and your family while you identify and move to a job more aligned with your Ideal Career Description. In order to ensure this move upward actually takes place, you must avoid the nurse's job search mistake number two.

2.) Do *not* search for a new job the same way you applied to nursing school.

If you do, your success in finding a better position in your search will rely purely on luck. Here is what I mean.

Most of us learn how to search for and obtain a new job position using the template of the methods we used to get into nursing school. Big mistake!

Remember back then. We were basically doing anything we could to get accepted. We were doing the interview equivalent of jumping up and down and shouting, "Pick me, pick me!" You were doing anything you could to get *them* to pick *you*.

That is *not* what this job search will be about.

In fact, a healthy job search turns the tables 180 degrees—it is another Mind Flip.

Turn the tables

In your search for your next position, make sure this job is a better match with your Ideal Practice Description than where you are now.

- You are not trying to get *them* to pick *you*.
- You are working to figure out if *you* will pick *them*.

Remember the "out of the frying pan and into the fire" clients I mentioned above? The mistake they made was remaining focused on what they didn't like about their current position and running away from these problems. They focused on getting a new employer to pick them and jumped as soon as a job became available. They were rarely lucky enough to stumble into a situation that was a good match for their Ideal Career Description.

A high quality job search

A high quality job search relies on you being crystal clear about your Ideal Career Description. With your ICD in hand, you can focus all your screening and interview efforts on finding a good match. Now *you* are screening *them*.

I have to repeat this because it is so important.

- You must know what you are looking for *first*.

- Ask the questions required to *screen them* …
- To see if they match your Ideal Career Description …
- To decide if *you* will pick *them*.

In your job search, you will use your ICD to generate your interview question set and take those questions with you when you go on your site visit.

- When you return home, you can sit down and build the Venn of Happiness for this job opportunity.
- You will understand just how much overlap there is between this job and your Ideal Career.
- Then, only one decision remains. Ask yourself, "Is this overlap enough to take this job?"

You are picking them at the end of a high-quality job search focused on finding a better match with your Ideal Career Description. In this case, there will be no jumping into the fire.

Now, you may worry about the fact that you are not working to get them to pick you. Let me be of some reassurance here. When you organize your job search and interview questions around your ICD, I have never known a nurse to find a job she wanted to take where she was not offered the position. Most likely, you will be complimented on your preparation. Your awareness and focus will impress them, and you will get the contract.

CHAPTER 7

YOUR EXIT STRATEGY

Making Room for What Comes Next

"Life is no brief candle to me. It is a sort of splendid torch which I have got a hold of for the moment, and I want to make it burn as brightly as possible before handing it on to future generations."
—George Bernard Shaw

"The young man knows the rules, but the old man knows the exceptions."
—Oliver Wendell Holmes, Sr.

For many of us, nursing has become part of our identity. In fact, many nurses feel a calling to enter the profession at a very early age.

Maybe something happened in childhood, like falling off of a horse at camp and having the nurse take care of you (one story I have heard in a nurse interview before). Whatever happened, you decided then and there you wanted to become one too.

Then what happens? We enter our nursing careers, often straight out of nursing school. We work long hours for years on end. Most of the nurses who go through my programs and read my books tell me they have been nurses for twenty-seven, thirty-eight, or even forty-five years! It becomes part of our lives.

So, it's no wonder that when we start to think about what else we may want to do with our lives, we find we actually have no answers to these types of questions. Retirement never crosses our minds.

I encourage you to figure out your Exit Strategy from nursing now, so you don't miss it when you get there.

WHAT IS YOUR EXIT STRATEGY?

You might think of it this way:

- Your decision to become a nurse opened a frame—the frame of what you hoped would be an extraordinary picture.

- You paint the picture from the bottom up, on purpose, from the palette of your Ideal Career, your Bucket List, and the family you will leave behind when you are gone.
- Your Exit Strategy completes the frame on this picture.
- Your Exit Strategy leaves you free to move on to your next art project, not simple retirement. This is a new frame on a new picture. I wonder what that vision is for you. Your Exit Strategy closes this frame and invites the next picture to form.

For most, your Exit Strategy is triggered by a financial threshold.

As much as we might hold our career as a calling, an art, and a science, when you no longer need to work to make the money to support your lifestyle, you cross a very significant threshold. This is a place where you are financially free. When you cross this threshold, you work because you *want* to, not because you *have* to. If you don't want to work anymore, you don't have to.

Know your number

If a significant portion of your Exit Strategy is reaching a financial goal, I encourage you to put some concrete numbers on that goal now. Whether you are just starting in your career or have been working as a nurse for thirty years, know the exact net worth number you are using as your target. Regularly check your progress toward your goal.

Hire a fee-based financial planner, and meet with him or her no less than every third year. Know your goals and your progress toward them. This is another place where you can acknowledge and celebrate your progress. Treat yourself like a dog for any progress toward your target net worth. You deserve it.

Financial questions are a core component of my initial conversation with nurses. A fascinating component of those consults is how infrequently nurses know their net worth. Most of the time, they are afraid to know the actual number. They fear they are not saving adequately and would rather not know at all than be disappointed.

For the majority of my clients, one of my first recommendations is that they visit a financial planner and begin using him or her as one of their trusted advisors going forward. For almost all who follow that recommendation, they are surprised when their net worth is finally calculated. Eight times out of ten, they are actually doing better than expected and are so relieved they actually sleep better at night...

For some, they realize they are actually financially free right now and this can be a time to exercise their Exit Strategy. They can close the frame, celebrate all the experiences and lessons learned on the journey, and move on.

RETIREMENT HEAD TRASH

For most nurses, a whole new flavor of head trash comes up at the mention of retirement. Let's name it now so you can recognize, get rid of it, and make some room for a fresh, new, retired version of you.

A common voice in your head says, "I don't want to stop being a nurse."

I have news for you: you never stop being a nurse. Your worldview, your skills and experience, the letters after your name … they never go away. You will be a nurse until your last breath—trust me on this.

Fortunately, your nurse instincts are a universal skill set in the non-medical world. You are superb at assessing a situation and carrying out an appropriate treatment for almost any problem in almost any setting. If you sit on the PTA at your children's school, volunteer as a medical missionary, or someone asks you to be on the board of a local company, the organization is richer for having you there. Your nurse-ness adds to the discussion. You will find people seek out your opinion because of the value your nurse's perspective brings to the discussion.

Another common voice says something like, "What would I do with myself? I would just get bored."

I say balderdash. That's just head trash. Bored is a choice. Now, you get to reset your self-worth to match the quality of your time rather than the quantity of your actions.

There is an adjustment period, for sure. There will be months of adjusting to being in complete charge of your schedule. You will find a way to make a contribution to your family and community that matches the same sense of purpose you found in your nursing career. You will also find new activities capable of holding your passion and enthusiasm once your career is not dominating your time and energy.

All of a sudden, it is as if that 800-pound gorilla has been sent to a wildlife farm in the country and you have your whole "house" all to yourself again. It takes a little getting used to, but you can handle it.

An Ideal Retirement Description is in order

Just like the Ideal Career Description can be used to become much more on purpose about your career, you can build an Ideal Retirement Description and use it in exactly the same way. You might even want to switch the word Retirement for one of your choice. However you describe this next phase, what is your vision for the ideal situation? Write it down and put it in a folder. This is your new target.

Even if you are not working, you can continue to use your weekly strategy session to build a more ideal life here in your next phase. There is never a bad time to live your life on purpose. Now, you have much more bandwidth and time available to you to practice these skills and smile as you reap the benefits.

The energy of contentment

Before we end this chapter on your Exit Strategy, let me share the following observation about slowing down. I want to tell you something that I hope gives you confidence as you contemplate letting go of your identity as a practicing nurse.

I have found this to be true in my life. Check it out and see if you notice it too.

When I was working, there was always a certain frantic energy to working my shift. No matter how smooth the day went, unexpected things would pop up. We swam in a constant stream of busyness. Things stacked up, and we worked through them. We got behind, and we caught up. As a charge nurse, people approached from all directions to ask a question or get the status of the unit. It felt good to be the center of attention. There was a certain satisfaction in getting the work done. It was a high frequency buzz of being productive and plowing through the work.

If someone had asked me in that moment, "Are you happy?" it would have seemed a silly question to me. I was busy, productive, and getting the work done. Happiness had nothing to do with it. I was at work.

It was quite addictive, though.

If the work slowed down below a certain threshold, I felt unproductive. I would look for things to do rather than just sit around. Guilt would creep in around the edges. I was "jonesing" to be busy.

Fast forward to after I quit my job.

My days were no longer ruled by my unit or the shifts I worked. It took a while to let go of the hunger to be productive and do lots of things. I missed people coming to me and asking all sorts of questions, being the boss, and telling them what to do. I realized that I was sometimes doing things just to keep busy.

As time wore on, I found myself getting move involved in my garden. I created a beautiful indoor sanctuary of cacti and a perennial garden outside my living room bay window. In the mornings as I ate my breakfast (something I never even did when I worked on my nursing unit!), I realized that I enjoyed simply sitting and watching the plants. Sure, they weren't doing anything that I could see with the naked eye, but that gentle, calm stillness was totally enjoyable to me.

It was a sense of satisfaction, similar to the one of having a productive day at the office … only on a completely different wavelength. This was quieter, lower frequency, calm and relaxed. I could breathe into it to make it more vivid in my awareness. Still, it took me several minutes to recognize its essence.

This was happiness. This was contentment.

As I sat in stillness, I realized up until now I had always hoped to construct this feeling by working hard enough, seeing enough patients, making enough money, and being a good nurse. I had been conditioned to believe happiness is something I earned or I put together piece by piece. If I was busy enough, productive enough, and brought home enough, I would end up being happy too. What all this activity earned me was the satisfaction of being productive.

This feeling was very different.

It did not require effort. In fact, it appeared to be something that was present in the background of my awareness all the time. I had to step away from my career and slow down for several months to be able to feel it clearly.

It was not a total stranger, though. I recognized it as something I had felt in fleeting moments during my career—on a weekend when I was rounding with the on-call attending or in the moments spent away from work with my husband.

Now, in the relative peace of being a nurse who is no longer working full-time on a nursing unit, this feeling is available full flow, straight from the tap, anytime I want.

Check this out for yourself in a quiet moment.

Do you feel it? Is happiness and contentment there for you in the background? I encourage you to take a deep breath and invite it to sit a while with you. One way to invite it in is to practice the Satisfaction Mind Flip (Chapter 2) and count your blessings.

Right now, you can practice breathing and relaxing into the things that are going right in your life. Get familiar with the energy of happiness and contentment so you recognize it when it tries to get your attention.

Last but not least, I want you to know that much more of this feeling is available when you activate your Exit Strategy by stepping away from your career and into your next phase. Here, you will have the space, time, and energy to become very familiar with happiness again—just like you were when you were a child.

You can relax and stop trying to earn it.

You will cock your head like a curious dog and then smile when you have finally slowed down enough to realize it is all around you, even now.

Exit Strategy ACTION STEPS

- Consult a financial advisor and create your retirement plan.
- Visit your financial advisor now and at least every three years going forward to measure and celebrate your progress.
- Know when you cross the threshold of financial freedom, and understand at that point that you only work now because you want to, not because you have to.
- Create an Ideal Retirement Description and review it at least monthly.
- Use weekly Strategy Sessions (with a cup of tea on a Sunday morning, perhaps) and your Ideal Retirement Description to create a new and beautiful picture in this next phase of your life.
- Practice the Satisfaction Mind Flip now to recognize happiness and contentment and develop the habit of noticing it all around you.
- Journal on your experience.

CHAPTER 8

CASE STUDIES

T he following case studies illustrate how three nurses, in very different circumstances, managed to create a more ideal life and ideal practice for themselves. My intention is to show you the universal nature of the tools above and the variety of ways they can be put to productive use.

FROM FRUSTRATED TO FULFILLED: PROFESSIONAL CONFIDENCE AND PERSONAL JOY

When I met Nurse B, she was stuck with a new manager who had a habit of putting B down. Despite Nurse B's thirty-five years of experience, she was being overlooked as her manager put new graduate nurses into charge nurse roles because they "were full-time employees." This frustrated Nurse B, as these full timers only worked one more day a week than she did.

Nurse B's manager took other responsibilities away from her as well. She wasn't allowed to orient new graduates or precept nurses on her unit. Other things, like committee work, were being given to other colleagues instead of her. This got to the point that Nurse B started to question her skills, abilities, and judgement. This pressure at work led to an increased stress level on the job and at home.

The first thing Nurse B realized during our work together was probably one of the most important realizations of her life. She told me one day, "There is nothing wrong with my nursing skills, abilities, or judgements. I can't worry about what others think of me. Just because someone has decided that they prefer someone else over me doesn't mean I am any less of a nurse."

As we continued our work together, Nurse B discovered that she is, in fact, still the same nurse she was when she started out—only better. She is more confident, feels empowered, and knows that she is a great nurse.

In addition to receiving a renewed sense of self-esteem and worth, when Nurse B applied the tools taught in this book, she reported feeling calmer. She is now able to take breaks from work, use breathing techniques to relax, gather her thoughts, and regroup. She reports the most important thing she has learned is how to "calm her soul."

183

Nurse B now feels a lot less stressed. She is able to walk away from a toxic work situation for a few minutes and gather herself. She happily reports these brief moments refresh her, allowing her to go back and continue her work with a positive approach.

Nurse B has also seen improvements outside of the workplace. The new confidence she has enjoyed on the job has spilled into her personal life. She feels more confident in her everyday abilities and actions. She feels more equipped to help others in her family and do the things she enjoys again, without feeling guilty. In fact, when asked what one of her favorite insights has been, she said, "I have learned along the way that we can work and have fun at the same time. Work and fun *do* go hand-in-hand!"

Most recently, Nurse B has reflected on the fact that she feels happier and more relaxed and enjoys work. She has gotten to know herself better and has learned how to go to a place of calm when needed. Nurse B has been pleasantly surprised how she has even been able to get along with the most difficult coworkers. She now has the tools to work out differences of opinion in a cohesive and agreeable way. Nurse B says, "I definitely get along better with everyone I come to in contact with, even family!"

MAKING A CAREER CHANGE AND STAYING COMMITTED TO SELF

When I met Nurse S, she was unable to make time for herself. Her job was so busy and time-consuming, she was unable to sustain a healthy life outside of work. Even though she worked at home, she felt as though she was working all of the time and unable to catch up. Nurse S needed motivation and support to make change.

What Nurse S was looking for most was help with work-life balance. She needed to simplify her life in order to enjoy her work. Nurse S was also possibly interested in a career change, thinking that might decrease her stress and increase her healthy habits.

When we started working together, Nurse S was pleasantly surprised at how easy the changes were. She already knew intellectually what to do. She just needed support to take the actions required to get different results in her life.

Nurse S quickly began to get more organized. She stayed committed by setting goals and sticking to them. She also opened up to breathing techniques and meditation and was able to relax and decrease her anxiety around trying new things.

A few months after we started working together, Nurse S enjoyed an enormous success. She reported back, "I was actually able to make a job change. I made the leap to becoming a nurse contractor! I am able to pick and choose assignments and work when I want to, thereby giving me more free time."

This was a huge win for Nurse S, as her professional change has impacted her personal life. She shared with me that she also made some health changes. She's lowered her blood pressure and cholesterol and has even lost ten pounds! When I asked her how she thinks she's been able to do this, she responded, "I take things one day at a time."

And even though she gives the tools in *Stop Nurse Burnout* a lot of the credit for her recovery from burnout, I remind Nurse S that she made these changes by blocking off the time for herself and staying committed. Taking the information and actually turning it into different actions was what provided Nurse S with the work-life balance she was longing for.

A LOST NURSE ON MEDICAL LEAVE FINDS HIS WAY

When I met Nurse K, he was on medical leave, awaiting surgery. At the time, he admitted to feeling completely lost.

As a workaholic who completely identified with his career and professional status, his brain was muddled. He often felt cranky and was unable to focus. Many times, he couldn't even sit down to read or watch TV. It was extremely difficult for Nurse K to share his thoughts or feelings.

This forced time off from work left Nurse K with no real sense of involvement in anything. When he came to me, Nurse K was knee deep in a personal and professional identity crisis. In fact, he shared, "If I'm not Nurse K, the director of a resident care facility, who the hell am I?"

As we began working together, Nurse K realized that he wasn't simply defined by the confines of what he could or could not do. He was pleased to learn that the profession of nursing had much broader boundaries with many alternatives. There were positions he never even considered, many within a subset of skills and abilities he already possessed, honed, and even practiced over the years.

When Nurse K discovered the power within himself, it was as though a dam opened. He once described to me that all of the pressure was released. Where he had previously felt trapped, jammed into a corner with nowhere to turn, he suddenly became aware of the many options that were available. Nurse K happily told me, "I know now that I don't need to remain where I am … unless I want to!"

It was thrilling to watch Nurse K open up to the various options available in nursing. He was also pleasantly surprised to find out that many other nurses have done a variety of things in our profession. There was a sense of freedom, he told me, as he started to choose and explore. The greatest insight for Nurse K was that he had a choice. He could do something with his nursing career; he could do what he wanted to do.

In our most recent time together, Nurse K shared the many gifts he has received from working with the tools in *Stop Nurse Burnout*. He most enjoyed the ease of access, saying, "These resources are so available to me. With multiple sources of content, the information is always right on hand." Nurse K has also commented on how inspired he feels. Engaging in interactions with nurses across the country, both on and offline, has instilled in him a sense of collaboration that has renewed his pride in the nursing profession. He feels certain that when he returns to work, it will not take over his life again.

CHAPTER 9

NEXT STEPS

Walking Your Path

"You have brains in your head. You have feet in your shoes. You can steer yourself in any direction you choose. You're on your own, and you know what you know. And you are the person who'll decide where to go."
—Dr. Seuss

"I shall be telling this with a sigh
Somewhere ages and ages hence:
Two roads diverged in a wood, and I—
I took the one less traveled by,
And that has made all the difference."
—Robert Frost

"Nothing in the universe can stop you from letting go and starting over."
—Guy Finley

Burnout's highest and best use is to show you the fork in your road—to point you toward the alternate path that has always been available. Burnout pushes you to live your life more on purpose from this point forward. Burnout done well is a turning point you will look back on and smile about, because this was the time when everything changed for the better. This was when you took the road less traveled by and that made all the difference.

LET'S REVIEW

I hope you understand burnout now in a whole new way. Perhaps you see it clearly for the first time.

- You understand burnout's causes, effects, and pathophysiology
- You see the programming of our nursing education and the traps it sets in your awareness
- You can recognize and take out your Head Trash.

- You have the structures to guide your own recovery from burnout and map a path to your Ideal Career.
  - ➤ Your Ideal Career Description
  - ➤ The Venn of Happiness
  - ➤ Your Master Plan
- You understand the structure of a weekly Strategy Session to put all this learning to good use
- You have learned a number of field-tested tools to lower your stress and assist you on your journey.
- We have shared leadership tools, so you don't have to work so hard and tools to get more of what you want within a bureaucracy.
- We have talked about the structure of an Ideal Job Search.
- You have gained clarity on your Exit Strategy.

Now it's your turn. Time to take action.

Remember back to the introduction. Recall Einstein's definition of insanity.

"Insanity is doing the same things over and over and expecting a different result."[16]
—*Albert Einstein*

No matter how much you understand about the concepts contained in this book, nothing will change unless and until you take action.

The only way to obtain *new results* in your life is by taking *new actions*.

You hold in your hands the escape hatch on Einstein's Insanity Trap. This is an authentic opportunity for you to live with purpose. I encourage you to use these tools to build your own Ideal Career and a rich, juicy, fulfilling life for yourself and your family.

You deserve it.

Now is your time.

ADDITIONAL RESOURCES

More Power Tools to Stop Nurse Burnout

I hope you have enjoyed this taste of the resources and support available in our coaching, live trainings, and consultation services. Don't stop here. Use this book to build a more Ideal Career and please come visit us on the web. All of the following additional Stop Nurse Burnout tools are available FREE at our website *www.StopNurseBurnout.com/powertools*.

The *Stop Nurse Burnout* Field Manual

- A printable workbook containing the summaries and action steps from each chapter and section above. It also contains blank documents for your:
  - ➤ Ideal Job Description
  - ➤ Venn of Happiness
  - ➤ Master Plan
  - ➤ Strategy Session Template
- You can download the document to your computer and print off as many copies as you need for as long as you wish into the future.

The *Stop Nurse Burnout* Newsletter

- Twice-a-month updates on the latest tools that are working now for real nurses in the real world to prevent burnout and build your Ideal Career.

Additional FREE Resources include:

- **Satisfaction Mind Flip Report**
  - ➤ Mini-training on the Satisfaction Mind Flip technique to focus on what is going right in your life.
- **Manage Your Boss Worksheet**
  - ➤ Full training on how to manage your boss, including the entire question set for your conversations.
- **Team Huddle Power Training**
  - ➤ Video training on the fine points of a well-run BID Team Huddle.

- **Team Problem Solving Protocol**
  - ‣ The Team Leader questions to use when your team is solving a problem in your practice.
- **Universal Upset Person Protocol**
  - ‣ Video training on how to deal efficiently, effectively, and empathetically with an upset or angry patient. Perfect to share with your entire team.
- **Recommended Reading List**
  - ‣ A list of my favorite books on leadership, communication skills, onboarding, and more

Use the following link to plug yourself into all these resources in the Power Tools Library at our support website. All of these additional Power Tools are free and my gift to you as an owner of this book:

www.StopNurseBurnout.com/powertools.

I wish you all the best in your journey to a more Ideal Career. If you have any questions, suggestions, or comments about the contents of this book, the Power Tools Library, or your own personal situation, you can reach me at *www.StopNurse-Burnout.com/contact.*

Keep breathing, and have a great rest of your day,

Elizabeth

Elizabeth Scala MSN/MBA, RN

StopNurseBurnout.com

ABOUT THE AUTHOR

ELIZABETH SCALA, MSN/MBA, RN is on a mission to shift the profession of nursing from the inside out. Nurses typically enter their careers with a desire to provide compassionate, heart-based care. Challenged by regulations, financial pressures, and technological advancements, today's nurse struggles to balance the art with the science of nursing.

As a keynote speaker, bestselling author, and virtual conference host, Elizabeth inspires nursing teams to reconnect with the passionate and fulfilling joy that once called them to their roles. Elizabeth is also a Reiki Master Teacher and Certified Coach.

Her articles are frequently posted on NurseTogether.com, Scrubsmag.com, onlinenursepractitionerprograms.com, and other nurse-oriented websites. She has consulted with or been a featured speaker for the South Dakota Nurse's Association, the Wyoming Nurse's Association, the American Holistic Nurse's Association, and many more.

She is also the host of two popular nursing podcasts. Elizabeth co-hosts the highly acclaimed RNFM Radio Show as well as her own nursing career podcast, Your Next Shift.

She lives in Maryland with her supportive husband and playfully silly pit bull. When Elizabeth is not speaking to or teaching other nurses, you can find her practicing yoga, playing in nature, or dancing to her favorite jam band, moe. You can reach Elizabeth via the web contact form at elizabethscala.com/contact.

ENDNOTES

1. Aiken, L et al. (2001) Nurses' report on hospital care in five countries. *Health Affairs*, 20(3):43-53.

2. There is very little evidence that Einstein ever said this. Nevertheless, it is absolutely true.

3. McHugh, M. et al. (2011). "Nurses' Widespread Job Dissatisfaction, Burnout, and Frustration with Health Benefits Signal Problems for Patient Care." *Health Affairs* 30, 202-210.

4. Aiken, L et al. (2002). "Hospital Nurse Staffing and Patient Mortality, Nurse Burnout, and Job Dissatisfaction." *The Journal of the American Medical Association*, 288, 1987-1993.

5. Houkes, I. et al. "Development of burnout over time and the causal order of the three dimensions of burnout among male and female GPs. A three-wave panel study." *BMC Public Health*. 2011; 11:240.

6. These tools are the basis of the Organizational Development philosophy of "Appreciative Inquiry" and the parenting philosophy of "Catch your kids doing something right." Also, see the questions in the book *First Break all the Rules*, referenced below. Most of all, though, try these tools out in your own life and see what changes.

7. Buckingham, M. and C. Coffman. *First Break All the Rules: What the World's Greatest Managers Do Differently*. Simon & Shuster, 1999.

8. Yee T, et al (2012). "The influence of integrated electronic medical records and computerized nursing notes on nurses' time spent in documentation." *Computers, Informatics Nursing*, 30, 287-292.

9. Hripcsak G. et al (2011). "Use of electronic clinical documentation: time spent and team interactions." *Journal of American Medical Informatics Association*, 18, 112-117.

10. Monarch K. (2007). "Documentation, part 1: principles for self-protection. Preserve the medical record—and defend yourself." *The American Journal of Nursing*, 107, 58-60.

11. Stokowski, L.A. (2013). Electronic Nursing Documentation: Charting New Territory. Medscape. Sep 12, 2013

12. Better!

13. Bodenheimer, T. & Sinsky, C. (2014) From Triple to Quadruple Aim: Care of the Patient Requires Care of the Provider. *Annals of Family Medicine*, 12(6), 573-576.

14. Bronson, P. and A. Merryman. *NurtureShock: New Thinking About Children*. Twelve Publishers, 2011.

15. Buckingham, M. and C. Coffman. *First Break All the Rules: What the World's Greatest Managers Do Differently*. Simon & Shuster, 1999.

16. There is very little evidence that Einstein ever said this. Nevertheless, it is absolutely true.

111

Made in the USA
Columbia, SC
15 February 2018